DRAMA AND EDUCATION

WITHDRAWN

NEWMAN COLLEGE
BARTLEY GREEN
BIRMINGHAM, 32.

CLASS	375.792
ACCESSION	65672
AUTHOR	ALI

N 0026171 8

To
PAST AND PRESENT COLLEAGUES

NEWMAN COLLEGE

DRAMA
AND
EDUCATION

A. F. ALINGTON, M.A. (Oxon)
Lately Staff Inspector, H.M. Inspectorate

WITHDRAWN

ST. PETER'S COLLEGE LIBRARY SALTLEY
NEWMAN COLLEGE LIBRARY

BASIL BLACKWELL
OXFORD

© *Basil Blackwell and Mott, Ltd.*, 1961

First Printed 1961
Reprinted 1963
Reprinted 1966
Reprinted 1970

631   97280   3

PRINTED IN GREAT BRITAIN
BY A. T. BROOME AND SON, ST. CLEMENT'S, OXFORD
AND BOUND BY THE KEMP HALL BINDERY. OXFORD

CONTENTS

INTRODUCTION

There are many for whom drama in schools means a social occasion only (The School Play); there are many for whom drama in schools spells danger or ' a frill '. This book seeks to persuade the former and reassure the latter. It also tries to set forth some practical suggestions for a complete course in drama throughout the school years, together with an attempt to adumbrate an under-lying ' philosophy '. It is the result of many years spent in watch-ing dramatic work in schools, training colleges and other institu-tions concerned wholly or partly with education in England and Wales, and of discussing their work and other relevant matters with those concerned.

For many of the ideas contained in this book I am indebted to a number of people, too numerous to be mentioned individually. They include teachers, training college lecturers, staffs of the Schools and Colleges of speech and drama, county drama advisers, local education authority inspectors, university pro-fessors, evening institute instructors, members of the staffs of the B.B.C. and of the British Drama League, actors and pro-ducers, educationists from Europe and the Commonwealth, and, of course, recent colleagues in H.M. Inspectorate, to whom I owe most of all. Authors to whom I am indebted include Miss Marjorie Hourd, Mr. James Laver, Prof. Allardyce Nicoll. I gladly acknow-ledge my debt to them all. And I wish to thank especially my wife, and my friends, Miss Ruth Foster and Miss Alison Milne, for much sound advice.

CHAPTER I

DRAMA AND EDUCATION

Drama is one of the arts through the practice of which children may grow and mature as human beings. Through the creative aspect of dramatic work children may bring to birth that which is original (to them) from material which is old; through its interpretative aspect they may grow in sympathetic understanding of the world and of people by contact with good and suitable plays. Both aspects involve the whole person, body, mind, emotions, spirit; both are ultimately one; both may be vital to the development of children.

The aim of drama in school is not to train actors or producers, any more than the object of art lessons is to train painters or sculptors. Very few children will, in fact, become actors or painters, but most of them, by means of the practice of the arts, will be filled with riches and ' have life more abundantly '.

How, in fact, does the practice of the arts in general and drama in particular affect the development of children (or adults)?

The act of creation is to make something new (to the maker) out of that which is old. You can design and make a new type of table or chair based upon known ideas. The design is the creation by an artist, the making is skilled craftsmanship. The artist must be a good craftsman: the craftsman, however skilful, is not necessarily a creative artist. The artist has something personal to say; the craftsman, as such, has little or nothing personal to say.

The moment of creation comes with the sudden fusing of two (or more) elements to make something new, the combining of two or more patterns of ideas to make a fresh pattern of ideas. It is usually accompanied by intense happiness, and arrives unexpectedly. Male and female elements fuse together to conceive a new and unique human being. Uniqueness is a characteristic of a work of art. Watts is reputed to have observed the power by which steam from boiling water lifted the lid of a kettle and from these ideas suddenly conceived the new and unique idea of using the power of steam to drive an engine. Elgar, walking in the Malvern Hills, related the rise and fall of their contours to music and came home with the melody of the Enigma Variations; and, further, imagined variations to this melody in terms of his friends. At their own level children are as capable of this creation of something new from something old as are adults. But they need ' the seeing eye and the hearing ear '. The artist sees things differently. Where you and I might see a handsome blue curtain he will see a pattern of folds, an infinite variety of blueness, perhaps ' the absolute '. To his seeing of the curtains he will bring intense imagination, compounded in the main of a wealth of experience, his own and his ancestors', plus something indefinable and uniquely his— insight, vision, spirit.

But the ' old ' ideas must already exist in the mind or the sub-conscious mind, if something new is to be created from them. There will be patterns of ideas derived from personal experience of all kinds, and, deeper, elements from ancestral experience. Everything or anything is grist to the creative mill. In ' The Great Dictator ' Charlie Chaplin exploited brilliantly the simpler paraphernalia of the ruler, a globe of the earth, a train, a red carpet, the Fascist salute, as well as the humbler stock-in-trade of the barber. Children have had a certain amount of experience, both first-hand and vicarious, to draw on, but they do not often reflect upon it, as does the creative artist. This reflection upon experience, difficult though it may be to contrive practically, is one of the important activities of the mind which we do not yet encourage sufficiently in schools. It may lead to original (for the child) thinking and planning and imagining—to creation.

The formation of concepts or patterns of ideas may be an unconscious process. Your concept of the physical universe may be a whirling confusion; or it may be something far more precise. At any rate, it will have grown from your experience of learning, observation, thinking and reading, and be informed by imagination, which is itself rooted in experience. But this concept will not have been consciously shaped throughout the whole of its formation. Much of it will have been built up without you realising it. You may not often have wittingly said to yourself, ' Now, I must go on

thinking out my concept of the physical universe,' though doubt-
less physicists, mathematicians and astronomers frequently do so.
But it might have been the better for you had you reflected consciously upon this subject more often. Your concept might then
have been more exact, more vivid and more readily usable.
Infrequently used knowledge and thought tend to atrophy.

It is important, then, to promote in children the formation of
consciously realised (sometimes), steadily growing and widely
embracing patterns of ideas, which will consist of thoughts,
emotions, sensations and images. These patterns of ideas will
be the raw material of their creative thought and their creative
acts. The steady growth of their concepts will be partly through
additional experience of all kinds, with (it is hoped) reflection upon
such new experience. But it will also be through the perception of
relationships and associations.

We should attempt to train children, as far as we can, to see as
well as to look, to hear as well as to listen, to observe with knowledge and imagination; to perceive, to relate, to associate. As a
result of such training in accurate observation and reflection on
that observation, in the recording in language of that observation
and reflection, particularly by simile, metaphor and imagery, some
children who do not already possess them may acquire the ' seeing
eye ' and ' hearing ear ', as well as some facility for perceiving
relationships and associations. Wordsworth's physical eye saw
daffodils, and his ' seeing eye ' simultaneously saw them as ' a
host ', ' golden ', and similar to the stars of the Milky Way.
Plato demanded rhythm and harmony in education because,
amongst other benefits, they will inculcate ' the instinct of relationship ', upon which reason itself depends. Experience stabilised
and made definite by reflection, ever widening concepts, relationships and associations perceived, these are the old ideas from
which, mainly, the new may be formed.

These highly personal and individual faculties, whether trained
or not, are the very stuff of thought, of sensitivity to experience, of
imagination, of full living, of human personality and achievement.
Without them growth is stunted. They are evoked, confirmed and
developed by the practice of the creative arts.

Almost all children are blessed—or cursed—to a greater or less

degree with the faculty of forming mental concepts and images of
that which is not immediately present. That imagination can be a
curse is evident from the experience of many, notably certain
writers and painters. Whether imagination is more of a blessing
or a curse depends largely on what it throws up, as well as on the
general attitude of mind and will-power of the individual. In the
case of children all these three can be influenced to some extent;
we can provide significant and evocative experience for their
imagination to use, we can affect their attitude towards life and
people, and we can present opportunity for the exercise of the
will. The livelier the imagination, as a rule, the greater the
sensitivity and the greater the vulnerability. Sensitivity entails
suffering, as well as ecstasy or enjoyment, and may be either purely
subjective or partly objective also. Purely subjective enjoyment is
often contagious and delectable, but self-centred suffering dis-
seminates gloom. We have no right to guard children against the
appropriate (as we judge) quantity and quality of suffering—they
will have to endure it, anyway, however much we try to protect
them. But we can attempt to ensure that their suffering is not
overwhelming in amount or violence, and we can begin to suggest
to them a sensible, positive, constructive attitude towards it,
steering them away from such natural concomitants of suffering as
self-pity and undue introspection. Rare indeed are the parents
who do not instinctively over-protect their children, some to the
point of mollycoddling. The indulgent, lax parent has many a
delinquent to answer for. But, as usual, it is a delicate balance.
Sensitivity and suffering can bring growth and maturity, or they
can help to sink a child in the morasses of self-centred fantasy.
Our responsibility is grave. We talk glibly of ' stimulating the
imagination ', as if this was always intrinsically desirable. But
with the exceptional child, and the ordinary child on exceptional
occasions, and most children under an exceptionally stimulating
teacher, there is danger. (The thought of the young Shelley
taking part in an evocative improvisation is formidable). We say,
' the children get over-excited '. Excitement from time to time is
a tonic; so is champagne, but even those who can afford it would
not generally wish to drink champagne twice a day. Over-excite-
ment with children sometimes means near-hysteria and usually

entails temporary loss of self-control. Apart from other considerations, the practice of the arts, and especially drama, calls for self-control and self-discipline, if the result is to have quality. But dramatic work of quality is impossible unless the imagination is alight; and for most children most of the time the stimulation and ' feeding ' of the imagination will be positively beneficial. But we should realise that imagination can be an enemy as well as a friend.

There are other valid reasons for the practice of the arts; only a few can be discussed here.

Each art and every medium has its own specific disciplines. The sculptor is limited by the potentialities of clay, stone, marble, wood, and implements. Within these limitations he is magnificently free; indeed, his very restrictions enable the great sculptor to burst emotionally and spiritually out of his material bonds, so that he can force his marble to speak with overpowering eloquence. The inventor, the scientific researcher must obey laws before he can command elements. Drama has its own disciplines—physical, mental, emotional, moral. The actor must stand still when he is standing still. When he moves, he must move to the appointed position in the agreed manner. When he speaks, he must fit his voice to character and situation. He must learn and know his lines. He should arrive punctually for rehearsal. He must often go over and over the same bit at the behest of the producer, and he must often wait patiently for long periods of time. He must be prepared to subordinate himself for the sake of the scene or the play. Having, perhaps, put his own point of view, he must be ready to accept and abide loyally by a different point of view. He must reflect the emotions of the character which he is playing, at the same time restraining his own individuality, so that his character ' comes across ', not himself. He must discipline himself to convey the given emotional ' atmosphere ' at the correct moment. Most of these, and other, disciplines are as valid for boys and girls as for adults. And before they are ready for performances of plays, children will experience other forms of discipline in their dramatic enterprises. In improvisation and other earlier work there are, for example, the need for close co-operation with other members of the group and loyal implementation of

group decisions; the binding force of the agreed plot and characterisation; the need to obey some laws of dramatic construction
and a few simple techniques, so that the scene may be clear and
effective. The same necessity for clarity demands disciplined use
of the voice in speaking and of the body in movement. And there
are always the restrictions of time and space and subject. Most
rigorous of all, perhaps, there is the discipline of selection—selection of ideas and of the means of presenting those ideas lucidly
and convincingly. But within these, and other, limitations the child
is magnificently free. And he is willingly disciplined, for he is
helping to create something; and the act of creation brings
absorption, which means, as a rule, happiness, or the agreeable
agony of reaching a decision concerning a work of art. ' Service is
perfect freedom '; service to an ideal, an idea, a community, a
human being—or a work of art. The service of an art calls for
self-discipline, and it is a positive discipline—' thou shalt ', not
usually ' thou shalt not '. It is essential that children should
experience the positive, freedom-forging self-discipline demanded
by drama and other arts.

Most arts are individual pursuits. They are carried out by
oneself, for oneself, they are one's very own and nobody else
holds the responsibility for success or failure. Most children
enjoy this kind of individual play—for all art is a form of play,
agonising though it sometimes is. The intensely personal form of
play, which art is, forms a necessary counter-weight to the (increasing) number of organised activities—e.g. classwork, ' pro-
jects ', team-games—which school life imposes. And not only
school life: human life is being organised and regimented continuously in ever larger and larger syntheses and the individual is
in danger of becoming less and less significant. ' We are members
one of another,' it is true, and we develop mainly through contact
with others, but we are also always ourselves and we need time
occasionally to be as intensely ourselves as only the practice of an
art or some other creative work can assure. (Drama may be a
co-operative affair, but it is also an extremly individual affair).

Art is a statement of truth; truth as the artist sees it. It is
essential that children should have the opportunity for stating
truth as they see it, and that they should attempt to interpret

truth as others have expressed it in, for example, music and drama. Children make some contact with, for example, mathematical, scientific and historical truth; it is necessary that they should face artistic truth also.

It has been said that all art is anarchic. From one point of view this may be true. But the mystics of all religions have affirmed the unity of the universe and the one-ness of everything it contains. Interpretations of that unity must be attempts to unify, if they are to be truth. Art brings order from chaos, it unites apparently disparate objects into harmonious relationships. In ' The Inferno ' Dante condemns his vast rogues' gallery to the ordered medieval hierarchy of hell. A century later Chaucer brings together another, more attractive, collection of rogues and saints on their journey to Canterbury. Manet disposes essential elements of 19th century Paris on the harmonious canvas, ' Les Paveurs '. And so on. Our world is apparently chaotic; religion, art and science are the great unifying factors. Children have need of order, regularity, pattern and rhythm in their lives. Their life and ours is based on rhythm—breathing, the flow of the blood, the seasons of the year, growth, decay. Their lives should be ordered, and they should have opportunity to bring order to their own lives and to bring order to the phenomena which surround them. Ordering of their environment will include the ordering of ideas and the ordering of experience in works of art.

The creation of a work of art calls for selection, for re-combination of the selected elements—as well as for vision. You must decide what to reject, what to include and how to re-assemble it. This means continually coming to decisions—often an agonising process. You cannot write one sentence without making decisions for better or worse. The will is being continuously exercised. Applied to moral issues the exercise of the will is one of the qualities which make us ' little lower than the angels '. Children cannot have too much experience of exercising the will or of making decisions of great or little import, but decisions by which they must abide, once made. This is valuable educational experience, experience which the practice of the arts can provide in abundance; though not often related to moral issues.

The creation of a work of art confers a final and complete

responsibility. This responsibility is a powerful incentive to succeed, because the work involved becomes personal, ' one's own ', an extension of oneself. Appropriate responsibility is a sovereign means for maturing personality. Responsibility for other human beings is usually inappropriate for children, though it is forced on some at an early age, and very competently they manage as a rule.

The process of creating a work of art, however far from perfection the final product, usually brings utter absorption in the work in hand. The work of art itself is an intensely personal business; the artist is externalising himself. Yet, paradoxically, when most himself in creating, the artist becomes so utterly absorbed that he forgets himself completely. In this single-minded concentration, when the self is forgotten and time has ceased to exist, lies an unique kind of happiness, greater than any, perhaps, except the rapture of the mystic, the brief ecstasy of the lover. It is a foretaste of eternity. At their own (perhaps humbler) level children should have the opportunity to experience both this absorption and this happiness. When it is a matter of co-operating in the creation of a work of art—as may happen in drama—then the happiness and the concentration may be even more intense, because of the contribution of each participant, and because the whole is shared.

In ' The Republic ' (III, 401-2) Plato said, ' We attach such supreme importance to musical education ' (and he included poetry and the plastic arts) ' because rhythm and harmony sink most deeply into the recesses of the soul, and take most powerful hold of it, bringing gracefulness in the train, and making a man graceful if he be rightly nurtured, but if not, the reverse. . . . The absence of grace, and rhythm and harmony, is closely related to an evil style, and an evil character.'

But, unfortunately for education (until recently), the influence of Aristotle has been paramount, and logical, rationalistic ways of thought have driven out grace, rhythm and harmonious proportion as aims of living, and led to much restriction of expression of emotion and of imagination in children.

The art of drama may have all the above values, as well as others, some of which are peculiar to itself.

The essence of drama is communication: communication of players to each other, of players to audience, of author via players, producer and designers to public. Any kind of communication between human beings, particularly when concerned with significant ideas, may deepen and intensify human relationships; and, apart from divine relationship, human relationships are the paramount matters of our life. Further, drama consists fundamentally of human beings playing at being human beings (or humanised animals, gods, etc.); it should therefore lead gradually to increased interest in and understanding and accurate observation of other human beings. And it demands for its implementation sensitive co-operation between human beings.

Drama, and perhaps song, are the only arts which make use of the whole human being as their medium—spirit, mind, emotions, imagination, voice, body. If (in drama) the whole person is willingly employed in communicating a form of truth in words and movements of significance and perhaps of beauty, the experience may be of inestimable value.

Acting, mime, movement, if they are to be significant and express truth, must ' come from within '. There must be sincerity, genuineness, integrity. That which is false, sham, derivative will be immediately apparent to the perceptive. To be another you have to be truly yourself.

To produce or act a part effectively in a good play should entail wrestling with the whole text to force from it the last iota of truth, and then wrestling with yourself (at rehearsal) to communicate that truth to fellow players, and later to audience. And effective production and acting both demand a high degree of sensitivity towards others.

Acting necessitates ' team-work '. Fortunately, a school can be free from the ' star system ' and the search for ' star quality ' which bedevil the professional theatre. There need be no ' up-staging ', and everyone concerned can have the experience of subordinating himself, when necessary, for the benefit of the whole. Timely projection of the actor-in-character is demanded, not ' putting oneself over '. And everyone concerned from producer and chief actor to scene-shifter and programme-seller can feel with truth that they have a valuable part in the total production.

Above all, perhaps, drama is worth doing for its own sake and for no other reason.

Drama is both creation and creation-interpretation; but these benefits, and others, will be discussed later.

CHAPTER II

Drama by children is at least 400 years old. But recently attention has been centred mainly on ' creative ' as opposed to interpretative drama for children. Since the last war, especially, the interest in ' creative ' drama in schools has increased and it is still increasing, not only in Britain, but all over the world. Much thought and experiment is devoted to it, and very similar general conclusions emerge, whether in Birmingham or Chile. UNESCO concerns itself with children's drama, and other international conferences on this subject have taken place.

In England and Wales many institutions have a keen interest in drama by children. For example, there are the Schools and Colleges of speech and drama, the training colleges, the Educational Drama Association with its membership from all over the world, some local education authorities, often through their Drama Advisers, the British Drama League, and so on. The Ministry of Education has its drama panel which reviews the teaching and the state of drama in schools, training colleges and other institutions throughout England and Wales. Wales has produced a pamphlet on drama in its schools. There is growing interest in Scotland. Many of the above institutions organise courses for teachers on drama in schools. Documents and books concerned with education as a rule give drama, if not an honoured place, at least some recognition of its potentialities. In some schools in this country there is work of outstanding quality in drama, and many people from abroad come to see it.

Simultaneously, there has been an increased effort to ensure that children experience the ' live ' theatre and are not wholly dependent for their drama on television and the cinema. This, again, has spread over the world and particularly in Europe. In England there are a number of children's theatre companies, which play more or less regularly to children in theatres or schools.

' Creative ' drama has come to stay. Its influence on the interpretative drama which has existed in schools for centuries has been greatly beneficial. Its present position and effect in schools may be compared with the situation in painting in schools after the influence of Cizek, Viola and Marion Richardson had begun to spread.

Drama in schools exists as an art-form in its own right through the practice of which children may develop, and as a branch of English studies. These twin points of view will be considered separately.

It is remarkable how closely the development of dramatic work in schools follows that of the drama itself.

It is a truism that small children are primitive creatures. They are animists, ritualists, anthropomorphic. Their world is half magical. Animate objects have personalities, the inanimate may come to life at any moment. Anything may be menacing and so may have to be pacified or influenced and therefore imitated, or made one with yourself and so brought within your power. This is ' sympathetic magic ', and drama began with magic. Magic concerned the whole tribe (the more the magic-makers the greater the potency of the magic) the members of which would perform the same actions at the same time, developing a rhythm and harmony and so a dance form. Hunters dressed up in the skins of the animals which they wanted to kill and imitated their movements. They identified themselves with other creatures (or people) and this was drama, or dance. Later, specialists in the ritual developed (Kings) and the separation of those watching from those taking part in the ritual began. Later still, there was a special locality for the ritual. Propitiation of the dead began, and stories and myths about the dead ' heroes ' had a part in the ritual. Magic and religion were both associated with drama, and still are. An evocative combination of lighting, canvas, paint, imagination, effective actors and some good lines, and we are transported magically to Illyria.

In children's lives drama begins in play, which is partly magical propitiation of the menaces of a grown-up world, partly identification with an admired object, partly the search for and assurance of personal power, partly curiosity, and a great deal of imitation. Then in school time, besides organised drama, comes much ritualistic play, which has no audience, which is heroic and romantic, and which may be in a kind of dance form drawing largely on mime and movement. Later, group work begins and there is a definite and limited acting space, though still on an ' open stage '. Identification with specific characters outside the self develops, and later the definite separation into actors and audience, with perhaps an ' announcer ' linking them, as did the Greek chorus. Scenes may take place, perhaps simultaneously, on different acting spaces, like the medieval ' mansions '. The scenes children act are often as simple and episodic and the circumstances in which they act them as informal as some medieval plays. Sudden death is as popular with them as with the Elizabethans, and, like the Elizabethans, they can transform a bare playing-space into the Forest of Arden with a flick of the imagination. As children mature so does their drama, and the conditions in which it takes place become more complicated and more realistic. But the magic remains.

Drama has been a natural growth: children's experience of drama should be a natural growth too. It is not surprising that their progress in drama should recapitulate to some extent the development of the drama of their forebears. And it is folly that they should be denied the experience of this recapitulation, both for the sake of their work in drama and for the sake of their own maturation. But as a nation we fear drama. It is too close to the primitive, too sensational, too irrational, too shocking. We fear the magic, yet we are the prey of magic most days of our life. Religious services are based on magic (and drama), and religion rests on faith. Art is magic. Personal influence and attraction is magic. Much of applied psychology is magic. Advertising is magic. We flatter ourselves that we have grown out of make-believe; we must have everything proven before we can believe in it: but you cannot prove anything that is really worth proving. Scratch a Britisher and you find a puritan. Yet this country has the finest dramatic literature in the world and one of the greatest traditions of theatre; and drama and poetry (often in combination) are the great British arts. Drama, the acting of it and the watching of it, as well as the study of it, is a noble part of the heritage which we ought to hand on to our children. And they are already creating it in their play.

CHAPTER III

Creative drama in schools, for children from the age of 5 to boys and girls of 13, 14 or 15, may be artificially divided into four aspects—play, movement and mime, the various kinds of ' improvisation ', and scripted plays devised and written by children. These are artificial divisions, for drama is one; all its forms may be considered as play (recreation and re-creation); movement and often mime are essential preparations for and ingredients of improvised drama and children's scripted plays; and the latter may be the consummation of satisfying improvisation.

Play is a necessity for man. Children develop and learn through play. Play in various forms is the centre of life in Nursery and Infant Schools, and the core of work in drama in Infant Schools. It is a commonplace that children 'play out' emotional disturbances, and that by doing so they ' come to terms ' with that which has disturbed and that which has, perhaps, delighted them. Through symbolic representation they face up to their joys, fears, anxieties, and, by facing up to them, place them in controllable perspective. And they enjoy pretending to be adults. Parents, relations, teachers, doctors: schools, holidays, hospitals, etc., and the manifold situations suggested by them form the themes of children's play for generation after generation. Children derive great satisfaction from imitating and identifying themselves with the grown-up, and playing out grown-up themes. One of the strongest desires of most children is to be grown-up and to wield the grown-up's power. Most of their toys and games reflect adult life in a miniature form which they can control. They also possess a gift for mimicry which is one of their chief ways of learning, but which is both a help and a danger when they come to drama. The good mimic may taste success and come to rely on imitation alone.

One of the ways, then, in which the teacher of Infants can lay sound foundations for future work in drama (and other ' subjects ') is by providing plenty of opportunities and apparatus for play and, if necessary, ideas as a basis for play. The wise teacher will always

be prepared to suggest ideas to supplement and enrich the sometimes meagre ideas which form the background of children's play,
though many a child who is gifted with the power to bring imagination to bear on experience will need no help. Some teachers have
a sentimental attitude towards the play of young children and
consider it sacrosanct. Nothing could be more mistaken. Most
children's play will benefit from injections at the right moment of
ideas which will develop the children's own themes and will
stimulate further their imaginative thinking about these themes.
Even more fruitful will be the effect of the gifted teacher who, by
means of her own personality and wealth of resources, is able to
create the kind of situation in which ideas are born. Progress is
the key-note of play, as of drama. Increasingly mature play will
afford the players increasing satisfaction. This 'feeding' of ideas
to children is of prime importance in drama, as in all education—
ideas which they can use and by using tend to make 'their own'.
They must have ideas to write with, or paint with, or act with,
and their own experience and the number of their concepts are
liable to be limited.

Besides opportunities and ideas for play, the wise teacher will
provide costumes and properties—but not too many and not too
elaborate. The child with the expensive toys—motor-cars which
have everything except an internal combustion engine; the sleek,
well-sprung doll's pram, which is almost big enough to contain
a real baby—is no happier, apart from the first moments of
rapture, than the child who has to bring his imagination to bear
on an old soap box on wheels, or a one-armed doll and a few bits of
stuff from her mother's rag-bag. The parents who buy their
children expensive toys are, in fact, doing them a disservice by
inhibiting the full use of their imagination. The teacher who
provides bits of wood and material and odds and ends of crockery,
and helps the children to make such things as crowns or swords
for themselves benefits them far more. Many children, like
adult artists, become more absorbed in something that demands
real effort and play of the imagination than in something which is
'laid on' for them—and absorption in the creative is a beneficial
state.

Movement is often introduced into the school curriculum at a very early stage, usually in close relationship to music or physical education. It is initially a form of play, may develop out of play, and may lead to highly complicated forms of play such as dance and drama. In an increasing number of schools movement is a ' subject ', or art-form in its own right.

Movement is the basis of all work in drama. An attempt to state its aims (and perhaps, by implication, its definition also) must be made.

First, then, movement should help to produce functional fitness, by means of the parts of the body moving in harmony, and so induce good health, agility and general well-being.

Movement may make the functioning of the body more harmonious by fostering those qualities in which the body is deficient—for example, greater lightness of movement may be given to the heavy; more swiftness of movement to the slow. In short, a better balanced, more resourceful mode of movement may be induced, and, as a result, so closely knit are body, mind and emotions, a better balanced person may emerge.

Movement is a means of communication. No one can make any movement without conveying something of himself to those who have eyes to see. Movement, therefore, can be a means of expressing ideas, either for the purpose of sharing an experience, or for communicating ideas to an audience—usually in a dance or dance-mime-drama form. But it is also part—and an important part—of the way in which an actor communicates. Indeed, an appreciation of the different qualities of movement—slowness, quickness; heaviness, lightness; flexibility, directness, and so on —is essential to the actor wishing to convey a personality to an audience. The same will apply to children wishing to communicate the individuality of a character, or the ' atmosphere ' of a scene. There are, for example, the different uses of space which are appropriate to various moods, such as withdrawing inwards, sinking in despair, coming forward in a mood of generosity, lifting upward or bowing low in worship. Understanding, experience and practice of these qualities of movement will give to children a language of bodily movement to call upon, often unconsciously, in their work in drama.

Akin to expressive movement is mime: it is not easy to say where one ends and the other begins. Perhaps it would be an approximation to truth to state that expressive movement describes ideas or experience in abstract terms, whereas mime shows human experience in concrete terms, by representational movement. But mime is not mere imitation—even in so-called ' occupational mime ', it should be ' larger than life ' and the handling of imaginary objects should be sensitive to their imagined qualities. Mime must ' come from within ', the outward action must be the sign of an inward sincere emotion or feeling, genuinely imagined or experienced. It is drama without the spoken word. It is one of the bases of the actor's art. Movement, as has been suggested already, is also one of the bases of the actor's art, but movement leads logically to dance because it is abstract, not to drama.

The same idea might be communicated, though in different ways, by means of movement, mime or drama. For example, the idea of the fall of a tyrant might be conveyed in movement by showing one powerful character advancing with great strength against a cowering crowd; then the crowd growing in strength, advancing with power against the tyrant, and finally annihilating him by the totality of their strength so that he sinks to the ground. It might be shown in mime by the tyrant's presence at the shooting of a number of rebels; then the comrades of the dead come together, anger rises, and they set forth to overpower the tyrant; finally, they kill his guards and put him to death. The mime could be expanded, translated into words and acted as drama. Finally, the murder of Julius Caesar (act III scene I) shows the same idea in a play text.

CHAPTER IV

As at all stages, drama in Infant Schools will be at once a fulfilment and a preparation.

Music and movement lessons of the B.B.C. type have no dramatic purpose and cannot greatly assist work in movement, because the teacher in the studio cannot see the response of the children and cannot therefore fit her material or its possible spontaneous development to individual classes. The lessons are not designed for this purpose. They may, however, cause some loosening up of the children's bodies and harmonising of their movements, as well as stimulating imaginative movement, and to this extent, therefore, may have value as preparation for dramatic work. Children should have considerable experience of movement and acquire thereby an abundant language of movement on which they can draw during their work in dance and drama. And in addition, for purposes of drama, they will need movement which is closely related to and a preparation for the theme of the dramatic work in hand.

At this stage, and at any age when children begin work in drama, it is best that everyone should take part in everything all the time. If all are concerned then everyone will be simultaneously active, no one can feel left out, the self-conscious (if there are any) will be less conspicuous. More important, each child may unconsciously help others by his absorption in the job in hand and by the ideas which he spontaneously contributes during the action—for children readily catch from one another. Individuals though they are, these very young children may begin to be sensitive to others and to other groups of children. Dramatically and otherwise, they cannot begin to increase objective sensitivity too early. In evolution the race has not been to the swift, nor the battle to the strong—but to the sensitive.

The content of this co-operative enterprise in which they are all engaged is of course of first importance, and nothing is more suitable than for them to ' play out ' an appropriate story well known to them. This will, in fact, be an extension of some of their normal games, though it will relate to the imaginary rather than the realistic. To take (in outline) an example, ' The Sleeping Princess ' —a useful story as it contains so many ' crowd scenes '. There is, first of all, the christening of the Princess, with the King and Queen and all the courtiers, when the godmothers bring their gifts and their promises, and one foretells the pricking of the Princess's finger with a bodkin, the years of sleep and the final awakening by a Prince's kiss. Then comes the scene in which the Princess finds the old woman spinning, pricks her finger and the whole court falls asleep. (This can be a ' multiple ' scene, with the members of the court going about their normal affairs, while the Princess has her unfortunate adventure). Next, the scene 100 years later when the Prince and his companion hew their way to the palace through the thick undergrowth, while the court still sleeps, explore the palace, and find the Princess. Then the Prince kisses her and everyone awakes and goes on from where they left off 100 years before. Finally, the wedding and wedding feast of the Prince and Princess.

The procedure might be as follows—first, the teacher tells the story to the children; then the children would do some preliminary mime and movement (with relevant noises) connected with the story; then follows a short discussion on how they will play out the story, introduced by such questions as, ' what people shall we have in it? ' ' which bits of the story (or scenes) shall we act? '; next, each scene would be discussed briefly and then acted; finally, the whole story would be acted straight through.

The preliminary movement or mime (which everyone would do together), might include—bringing christening presents in procession; approaching and bowing or curtseying to the King and Queen; spinning (noises); the ways in which various characters will move (e.g. the King and Queen with dignity); the usual business of the people of the court, e.g. the cooks cooking, the housemaids sweeping, the scullions fetching water or hewing wood (noises), the guards marching up and down, the King and Queen interviewing ambassadors; the sudden falling asleep in the position they happened to be in (noises); the Prince and his companion cutting their way through the undergrowth (noises); the final awakening and going on with their normal business

(noises); the wedding procession (music, perhaps). Each of these
will entail definite movement qualities, according to the personality
or situation involved. The teacher who has no experience of
movement, as such, need not fear to do this preliminary work;
movements which are large, convincing, sensitive to the imaginary
material being handled, sincere, and the product of the imagination
will help to imbue the children with the story and equip them
with physical and mental ideas for its acting.

It is better that the teacher should tell, rather than read, the
story—the impact of the told story, with its personal contact, is
greater—and should tell it excitingly, but at the same time serenely,
so that the children are thrilled, but feel secure; can identify
themselves with the characters and adventure with them, but
know all the time that they are safe with Miss X—have it both
ways, in fact. This means that she must take some trouble in
preparation of the telling as well as of the acting of the story. A
good story told well enough to fire the children's imaginations is
half the battle won at the start. Most children are able freely to
identify themselves with the hero or heroine of a story and thus to
take the first step of the actor—self-identification with an imagined
character. Fortunately, there has been a recent revival of the
ancient art of story-telling in many training colleges: it is one of the
primary teacher's most effective accomplishments.

Here are one or two suggestions of stories which lend themselves to dramatisation by children in the Primary School. Some
will be suitable for Infants, some for Juniors of different ages: not
all of them have large ' casts '.

> King Grisly Beard.
> The Blue Light.
> Rumpelstiltskin.
> The Four Clever Brothers.
> The Giant and the three Golden Hairs.
> The Sleeping Beauty.
> Hansel and Gretel.
> The Twelve Dancing Princesses.
> The Elves and the Shoemaker.
> Frederick and Catherine.

The Golden Goose.
The Fisherman and his Wife.
Snow White and the Seven Dwarfs.
The Four Travelling Musicians.
The Snow Queen.
The Wizard of Oz.
The Princess and the Pea.
The Emperor's New Clothes.
The Princess and the Swineherd.
Pinocchio.
The Sorcerer's Apprentice.
The King of the Golden River.
The Three Wishes.
The Mermaid and the Simpleton.

' Tales from many Lands.'
' Old old Fairy Tales,' etc.

Japanese, Russian, Norse, Red Indian, etc., myths and legends,
Arthurian legends, Robin Hood stories.

Greek myths, e.g. Midas, Ceres and Persephone, Orpheus,
Perseus, Jason, Theseus, Hercules, Pandora, etc.
The Iliad, the Odyssey.

Historical stories, e.g. Guy Fawkes, Pocahontas,
Columbus, the Burghers of Calais, etc.

Narrative Poems, e.g. The Pied Piper, Hiawatha,
The Jackdaw of Rheims, Ballads.

Discussion of how the story is to be acted should be kept at
first to the bare but necessary minimum—the children will want
to act as soon as possible. And at first they may not have many
ideas to contribute. In fact, early discussions may be restricted
to the location in the room of the scene or scenes and of the various
incidents in them, and who is to play the parts. The chief parts
can be changed for each scene—most of the girls will want to be

the Princess and many of the boys the Prince in ' The Sleeping Princess '. In some scenes of some stories it is possible to have two or three children playing the same character in the same scene—e.g. it would be possible for several pairs of children to hack their way simultaneously through the undergrowth, without interfering with the action of the story or the children necessarily considering this inappropriate. But the actual organisation of the acting of the scenes may take rather longer, and if the acting is to be satisfying to the children, it is necessary that the organisation should be effective. At later stages of dramatic work increasingly greater responsibility for the devising and acting of the scenes will be thrown on to the children, but until they are ready for this responsibility it is a mistake to impose it. At first, many children will be happier under direction. This will also enable them to achieve better results and will therefore increase their confidence; and it will ensure discipline from the start. If not controlled and organised, children tend to become over-excited when they begin drama, discipline become difficult to maintain, the whole piece of work disintegrates, and no one is the happier, including the children. Firm (but genial) handling is necessary therefore at the outset; in due course the incentive and absorption of creative work and the discipline of the art itself should lessen the need for firmness. But drama is always liable to be dynamite.

In spite of the necessity for positive direction and organisation, however, children should never, at any stage, be told how to play a part. Instructions such as ' say it like this ', ' use your hands in this way ' restrict invention and turn the child into a mere puppet. Besides, many children will speak the words or do the action in their own way, which will be the most appropriate way for their purposes (not for the teacher's purposes), more effectively than any adult can show them. When she sees that a child needs help in order to achieve his own purposes, the teacher (as do many producers) should ' put him in the picture ' again, and allow him to work it out for himself. ' Look. You are a strong young man wanting to get to that Palace and find out what is inside. The undergrowth is very thick—bushes, brambles, nettles, saplings— but you have a sharp sword, and you are very strong and deter- mined '. And so on. If the picture is painted vividly, the child's

imagination will be stirred again, and the results, even from
unlikely children, may be astonishing.

It is possible, of course, that children will contribute plenty of
ideas from the start. It is advisable to try out as many of their
suggestions as time allows, even though they may seem indifferent,
provided that they are sincerely advanced. Few experiences are
more inhibiting than to have your suggestion brushed aside or
ignored; but if the suggestion has been tried and seen not to
work, the disappointment is not so keen. Besides, trial-and-error
often leads to success and is an effective way of learning. The main
difficulties with trial-and-error in dramatic work are the shortage
of time and the frustrating effect of holding up the acting. As
usual, the teacher has to compromise and assess continually the
state of mind of the class. Amongst the aims of the teacher in
this work should be the necessity for solid achievement within
each lesson, the need for steady progress, and the desirability of
keeping enthusiasm alive. But if the children have lost interest
in a story, it is fatal to continue with it.

This ' acted story ' (as it might be called) has taken many words
to describe, but such a story can be satisfactorily concluded in one
lesson, and, if possible, it is important that it should be timed to
last for one lesson only at this stage. Loose ends are unsatisfactory,
and an (unconscious) sense of unity matters to a child.

Drama in Infant Schools is sometimes considered in terms of
mime only, and mime at the superficial level of mere bodily action
devoid of any deeper significance; an instance of that major crime
of some teachers—under-rating the capabilities of children.
Speech may be positively forbidden. ' When you are doing mime
you must not speak.' The children may be bursting to speak, but
' We are doing mime and in mime you don't speak '. They
should be positively encouraged to speak when imaginatively
prompted to do so.

But there are occasions when mime is a better medium for
expressing ideas than spoken drama. For example, much satisfaction may come from a ballad which is read or spoken by, say,
two-thirds of the class while the other third mimes the actions
related. There is a school of thought, however, which holds
that the ballad, being an art-form in its own right, should not be

interpreted in another medium. Again, a fairly abstract theme
may be expressed more effectively in mime or movement rather
than spoken drama; for example, the coronation of a King, or a
rural scene, such as the home environment of Ruth, or the Prodigal
Son, or Joan of Arc. There are also the purely practical situations
when it is difficult or undesirable to introduce some ' prop ' and
therefore the children have to ' mime ' or pretend it. The children
should handle their invisible props with real imagination. If they
are sufficiently caught up in the imaginary situation, they will be
likely to do so, but they may need some practice in appreciating
physical qualities, such as weight or shape. These occasions are
the time for ' occupational ' mime; occasions linked with a specific
need. ' You have to crown the King. How big is the crown?
What is it made of? How heavy? What shape? How will you set
it on the King's head so that it sits comfortably and suitably? '
Occupational mime divorced from an imagined situation seems a
waste of time.

At the Infant School dramatic work will often be a mixture of
movement and mime, with some sound or speech spontaneously
added. Both speech and ' sound effects ' should be encouraged.
Though most children normally talk incessantly, they are sometimes shy of speaking before others. This difficulty can be overcome, if they are imaginatively involved in the situation which is
being interpreted, and if sufficiently cogent ideas for dialogue
have been suggested to them. Effective aids to speech for the
unforthcoming are sound—the making of abstract sounds, e.g.
rain and water noises during ' Noah ', or glacier noises in ' The
King of the Golden River '—and ' made-up ' words, e.g. ' scritch,
scratchle, scrabble ' for rat noises in ' The Pied Piper '. These
sounds will also be fun to make and should help to create ' atmosphere '. But often children will all talk at once. This does not
matter in the least, unless the development of the situation is held
up. But the fact that two or three are speaking simultaneously is
unimportant from the point of view of an audience, for there
should be no audience.

There should be no audience (and therefore no stage techniques). Performances to any kind of audience, except, perhaps,
to another class of contemporaries, are out of place in the Infant

School. For this is a form of play and almost as spontaneous as play, as laughing, as crying, as jumping up and down when you are pleased, as dancing or running for the sheer fun of the power and physical satisfaction of it. A performance almost inevitably implies some organisation of what is to be performed, and this may kill the spontaneity, however tactfully it is done. The drama of very young children must be allowed to flow on unhindered. Performances to adult audiences should be rigorously banned, even against pressure from parents. ' Oh, but the children enjoy it so! ' Of course they do. It is great fun. And why shouldn't they have enjoyment? Children enjoy most things, but enjoyment of itself is not necessarily a criterion of beneficial occupation, though for some teachers recently enjoyment has become an educational end instead of a means and a by-product. Most children can easily be lured into showing off before their parents and friends; and sometimes these performances are mainly showing off. The children are far too immature to become identified with a part or an imaginary situation on a public occasion, and acting to an audience is of no real benefit to a child, unless he is caught up in the play and unless he feels himself part of a team working on the play. Children are usually conscious of themselves, their costumes and their make-up, and they are conscious of their audience: it requires a more mature person to be conscious also of his own part, of the situation in the play, of the other characters he is playing with, and of the audience he is communicating to. Children are often capable of this later on, but not yet. Further, the children are usually drilled in their parts, their actions and their movements for a performance. The teacher responsible naturally wants ' to put on a good show ', and this often means to put on a good show according to adult standards, from the adult's point of view. Children are too frequently exploited to produce a parents' holiday. If the children's own effort, devised and worked out by them, is shown in performance, the temptation to ' improve' it (again, according to adult standards) is strong and the same exploitation may recur. Further, the adult audience brings an adult view-point to bear on the children's performance—the attitude of ' how sweet! ' And the point of view of the keen teacher is apt to be that summarized in the statement of one of their number to an H.M.I.—' Infants always let you down on the night '.

There are many teachers who would forcefully object to this wholesale condemnation of performances to adult audiences in Infant Schools, denying the truth of the arguments here adumbrated. The present writer believes that, with very few exceptions, a ban on performances to adults should apply to Junior as well as Infant Schools.

To obtain real satisfaction in dramatic work children must be absorbed in what they are doing. This absorption may be difficult to induce at their first introduction to drama, or at the beginning of a lesson devoted to mime or drama. There are various ways of overcoming this difficulty, some of which should be used sparingly. Appropriate music is one, percussion is another, the children's own use of sound a third. With these ' aids ' it is mainly strong rhythm which tends to produce relaxation of body, an easier flow of movement and, perhaps also, some release of emotion, all of which assist expression of ideas in dramatic or dance or movement form. We need not be too frightened of emotion in the class-room. After all, children can snap out of a mood in a split second when it has been engendered by and exists in the imagination and not in reality, though it may linger for a time in the memories of some. We allow children to be exposed quite often to crude emotions on T.V. or in the cinema, which they watch passively. In dramatic work in schools they will be concerned with emotion actively. Not that there will be a great deal of emotion in the kind of stories that form the basis of Infants' dramatic work, and what emotion there is will be of a simple, homely kind. Nevertheless, these aids should be discreetly used. Sentimentality and the emotional ' splurge ' must be avoided at all costs; and the sooner that children are able to become involved in an imagined situation without artificial assistance, the better.

[The simplest and most effective aids are the dressing-up box and props. The less elaborate these are, the more the children are able to bring their own imagination to bear on them, the better —the odd bits of material for cloaks or skirts, beads and rings, long sticks for spears, shorter ones for swords, cardboard crowns. Put a crown on his head and in a moment a child may become a King, with altered ways of movement and speaking, and he will remain ' in character ' for minutes on end. The dressing-up box will be used for children's own play, as well as for drama. Most of us enjoy dressing up and becoming someone else, or ourselves intensified. Firmly planted in fantasy, our ego happily ' massaged ', we burgeon. Provided that we can snap out of fantasy, as children can, and provided that our fantasy is based on reality (Kings are real people, though we can never become one, but ogres and space monsters are not), little harm results for us and probably much good for young children.

Ideally, space is essential for satisfactory dramatic work, so that the children can move freely, and so that various scenes can take place simultaneously, if necessary. The school hall is the proper place for drama, but if the hall is not available, what then? Most class-rooms nowadays are reasonably large and many contain reasonably mobile furniture. With a little training the children can clear a space in the middle of the room or to one side in a very short time. This space will be insufficient for much movement, but adequate for most dramatic work. It is important, if possible, that every member of the class should be actively absorbed in the work in hand. It is seldom satisfactory for part of an Infant class to be an audience, and it is almost certainly vain to hope for much helpful comment from them afterwards. But some class-rooms are too small and the furniture too heavy to be moved. What then? There is only ' the space in front ', the passages between the desks and, perhaps, the tops of desks as well. Sometimes there is out-of-doors.

The real solution to the problem of restricted space is not physical, but in the imagination. It lies in the quality of the material used for dramatic purposes and its effective presentation to the children. Given a gripping, absorbing story or other subject matter, evocatively presented, lack of space will not be invincible. The best work in any subject sometimes happens under the worst conditions. Absorption in the matter in hand will overcome many obstacles. Of course, the material must be very carefully chosen so that action may be satisfactorily fitted into the space available. Some solve the problems of too little space by getting small groups to play in turns, but group work should be a later development and children in the Infant School are usually too immature for it. This matter of confined space will be considered later.

Where there is plenty of room it is essential that the children should make full use of it. Rostra which are light enough for the children to handle and tough enough for them to move on are valuable aids and stimuli. In arranging them to suit their own purposes children become scenic designers. The rostra, appropriately arranged, may become a throne room, a fortress, a tower, a ship—the only limit is the imaginations of the children. They are gigantic bricks for children's play, and all the more stimulating for being large.

CHAPTER V

Many boys and girls of 9, 10 and 11 seem to be at a peak of development. They appear to reach a state of fulfilment (as children) which is unique. They may grow gradually into men and women of great integrity and distinction, but they can be, and often are, better at being children of 9, 10 and 11, so to speak, than they will be at being men and women of 40, 50 or 60. And the reverse is as often true, of course. But the important thing is that here, in the top half of Junior Schools, are children blessed with so many gifts and so many potentialties, and the best way in which we can serve them is to see that all these gifts and potentialities are realised to the fullest. By ensuring that they are most fully themselves at the present we shall prepare them best for the future. Education is only indirectly a ' preparation for life ': it is chiefly and directly the fulfilment of the present.

How can drama in all its aspects assist the development of these children, gifted or otherwise? And what gifts have they which can be particularly realised in dramatic work? The memories of children of this age are often at their best. Their minds are often alert, budding freshly, not yet over-clogged with useless knowledge. Almost all of them have an imagination which can range untrammelled over their own first-hand or vicarious experience. Some of them have ' the seeing eye ' and ' the hearing ear ' of the poet. Some are acutely sensitive, some are accurately observant within the limits of their own, often wide, interests. They are romantics. They are enthusiasts, devouringly curious, filled with wonder, hero-worshippers, tough, competent, filled with overflowing vitality. They can be devils and saints, tender and sadistic in the same minute. They know a great deal about the raw material of living. Their behaviour is instinctive, impulsive, and they can be ruthlessly selfish. They long to be grown up and, within appropriate limits, can be highly responsible people. They love and hate whole-heartedly, but deeply. The range of their competence is exceedingly wide. Unfortunately, this luxuriant promise is sometimes tarnished by varying degrees of physical, mental, emotional and spiritual ill-health, but at its best this is a glorious stage of life.

Certainly, creative drama is often at its highest in Junior Schools. Some of the work in drama in these schools compares favourably with the best original writing and painting by children of this age. This fine creative work in drama always has one or two characteristics in common, wherever the school may be—utter absorption and so a whole-hearted, serious, business-like attitude to the work in hand; free flowing movement; a flair for invention, often introducing and culminating in the unexpected; speech that is terse, forthright and incisive because the words are sincerely felt; results achieved most economically; little or no sense of an audience; growing sensitivity of the players towards each other; the fact that the ' first time through ' shows the creation at its best, and the fact that repetition always brings alteration even in words and movements intimately known—and, from the adult onlooker's point of view, forgetfulness after a while that these are children; the emotion that arises from seeing something done well; a sense that here is truth.

How to achieve these remarkable results? And, first, what is a valid progression in the forms of drama for the Junior School? —remembering that, as with any art, there are no right or wrong ways, no certain recipes for success. There is only truth or false-hood, as the artist or artists see it. What seems true and right to some may seem false and wrong to others. Remembering, too, that, as in every school enterprise, progress is essential and children should be faced, when ready, with ever more exacting demands.

Ideally, movement should continue as a regular feature of the curriculum—as in the Infant School—both movement of a general nature, and specific movement in preparation for a piece of dramatic work. Movement of a general nature should include the working out of ideas and themes of a dramatic or near-dramatic kind in terms of movement and mime, with sound added where necessary. One or two examples of such themes or ideas are— Festival, Coronation, the Nativity, Flood, Storm at Sea; Perse-phone, Orpheus and Eurydice, some of the adventures of Odys-seus; the Israelites in Egypt, the plagues, the flight from Egypt, the destruction of the Egyptians in the Red Sea; some of the adventures of Beowulf; the Song of Roland. It is impossible to over-emphasize the importance of this kind of movement at this stage, particularly. Mime should continue, too, both as preparation for and, perhaps, as an integral part of dramatic work. For the rest, the progression of work might be as follows.

Continuation of ' the acted story ', bringing in everybody all the time, as far as possible, as in the Infant School, but using stories and poems which make increasing demands on the children —a progression, for example, from a straightforward version of Noah and the Flood to the story of Joan of Arc, or Moses and the Golden Calf; or from Noah in its simplest form, with the children acting as the animals, to a version of Noah which emphasizes the attitude of Noah towards God, the conflicts between Noah and those who do not believe in his prophecies nor his attitude to God, and the conflicts between Noah and his blind and quarrelsome family.

Out of this acted story will bud naturally the next development —the acted story with certain parts of it worked out and acted by small groups of children; all the children, obviously, being included in one or other of the groups. But this advance should not be contemplated until the children are ready for it. They will be ready for it when they can contribute valid and workable ideas to the dramatising of a story, when they can give the character they are playing something of a personality (even if only a ' type '), when they can move and speak improvised dialogue with some conviction and confidence, and, above all, when they are able to become absorbed in the work. All this may take time, but the objective and sensitive teacher will know instinctively when they are ready to move on.

An example of group work ' budding out ' of an acted story— easy in some ways, hard in others—is The Prodigal Son. First scene. In mime and movement the whole class manifests the primitive agricultural and domestic background during, for example, spring. In this scene the elder son, with the father, is directing the agricultural operations competently and conscientiously, while the younger son is telling his mother that he is tired of life at home and wants to sample life in the great city. A family conference is held and the younger son leaves home with his

' substance '. Next, different groups are responsible for working
out and showing in separate scenes the younger son ' wasting his
substance in riotous living ', and being employed to look after the
pigs for a pittance during the famine. The ' riotous living ' need
not be wholesale debauchery: there are plenty of respectable ways
of losing one's money. The pig-minding scene, with its pricking
of conscience (' I will arise and go to my father . . . '), can be fitted
into its proper place later. There can be a different prodigal
son in each of these group scenes, and different ones also in the
first and last scenes. The whole class can take part in the scene
of the famine, which might well be done in movement, with the
scene of the prodigal son and the swine immediately after it, or,
perhaps, going on simultaneously. Finally, the scene of the return
of the prodigal, his glad reception, the behaviour of that rather
tragic figure, the elder son, and the feasting. (Of course, the whole
story could be treated in modern idiom).

The telling or revising of the story, the preparatory movement
and mime, the discussion and working out of the general scenes,
the discussion and working out by groups of the group scenes, and
the assembling of the whole acted story in a ' run-through '
may occupy several lessons. As long as the children are absorbed
in it, time will not greatly matter; but they will have to regain
concentration after each gap of time. Some movement exercises
should effect this.

After some experience of working in smaller groups to devise
scenes which will carry forward a particular story in which the
whole class is concerned, the next stage might be that of handing
over to the children a complete story, the different scenes of which
would be worked out by different groups and then acted consecutively to form a whole. Those not taking part in any given scene
could, if wanted, act as ' crowd ' under the direction of the producer of the scene in hand. The advantages of this kind of group
work are that occasionally everybody will be concerned in the
scenes of the other groups, but there will be important parts for
most of the class in their own scenes; everyone will see the scenes
of the other groups, and there may be different interpretations of
the same character or similar situations; the necessity, perhaps, for
linking the different scenes; the assumption of more or less

complete responsibility for the dramatisation of the story by the class.

The final stage of this process of the acted story which shades off gradually into group work might be to give the children the plot of a play (or story), discuss with them the scenes into which it may be divided, appoint groups for each scene, and then proceed as before. Some possible play plots (in their simplest forms) for this purpose are—'Macbeth', 'Julius Caesar', 'The Taming of the Shrew', 'Richard II', 'Richard III', both parts of 'Henry IV', 'Henry V', 'Twelfth Night', 'Hamlet', 'Coriolanus', 'The Tempest', 'Antigone', 'St. Joan', 'Tobias and the Angel', 'Great Expectations', 'The Count of Monte Cristo', 'The Speckled Band', 'The Hound of the Baskervilles' (and other Sherlock Holmes stories), 'The River Line', 'Noah' (Obey), '*Le Médecin malgré lui*', 'Cyrano de Bergerac', 'The Bells', 'The Devil's Disciple', 'Treasure Island', 'Round the World in 80 Days', and so on. It would be interesting afterwards to outline to them how Shakespeare and other authors in fact worked out their plots, and then, if the children were still interested, to ask them to act these authors' scenes in their own ways. This could be an introduction to some of the great playwrights—an introduction to be followed up later.

Before considering the kind of group work usually known as Improvisation, something must be said about the discussion of their drama work with the children. Preliminary discussion is particularly important when the bare outline of a plot only is given to the children, for with this stimulus alone they are dependent on their own imaginations for most of the detail and they may need some help.

Clearly, the more fruitful the ideas that the children have in mind before they start work, the better the quality of the drama that will result; but the sooner the children can start acting or working on their own, the better they will be pleased. Too much discussion before they take action will only lead to restlessness: the perfectionist in the class-room is often self-defeating. In the discussion before an acted story the sort of decisions that teacher and children together must reach are—What scenes shall the story be divided into? What characters shall we bring in? What are these characters like? How does character A get on with B, C with D, etc.? In this first scene, what will happen? Where in this room will this be acted? Which characters will be in this scene? Who will act them? How will they move, stand, sit? What sort of things will they say? It is advisable to discuss the acted story one scene at a time, play the scenes as soon as they are ready for acting, and finally run through all the scenes consecutively and without a break. In this way acting can begin at the earliest moment. It is advisable to do some preparatory movement or mime after the initial outlining of the plot and also before each scene, and to do it with everyone, even though the movement concerns one character only. It will be useful experience for everyone, and will help to give them all a 'feeling' for the scene. It may be wise to do this preparatory movement before casting, as the movement may show who is likely to play a given part effectively.

The discussion in answer to some such question as ' What sort of things will they say? ' may be particularly fruitful, for it may lead to argument as to whether suggested ' lines ' are true to the character concerned, and will give the teacher the opportunity to deprecate the too trivial or over-slangy, thus setting a standard of robust English. The thinking out and discussion of dialogue which is valid and significant for character and situation may be one of the most truly creative elements of the whole enterprise.

Discussion guided by the enthusiastic but thoughtful teacher can add much to the children's imaginative conception of story or plot, and with a tactful use of the Socratic method (especially, ' why? ') possible translations into action of story or plot will begin to come vividly to the children's minds in terms not only of mental pictures, but also of the actual circumstances in which they are to play it—in this room, with the teacher's desk as the Grand Inquisitor's table, the stake to be at the opposite end of the room, Marlene as Joan of Arc, Terry as the Executioner. The bare walls of the class-room may transform themselves gradually into the stone and Gothic arches of a medieval castle, the wood for the fire may be piled in readiness, Marlene's neat clothes and washed face may begin to assume the pallor and threadbare drabness of the incarcerated, and a black mask to cover the upper half of Terry's pink, chubby face.

' How do you think Joan would have been dressed? She had been in prison for months, in a cell in a high tower.'

' Sort of black and shabby . . . She always wore men's clothes, didn't she? '

' What would those who were trying her—Princes of the Church—what would they have thought of her answers to their questions? '

' Well, they thought they knew what God wanted, from the Bible and things, but she listened to the voices of the Saints.'

' How would she feel when threatened with being burnt alive? ' . . . and so on.

Within reason, the more experienced the children become, the more precise should be the details of the scenes. ' Oh well, he could do that somehow ' must quickly disappear. Over-precision will be merely stultifying, but words and actions which definitely affect the plot will need to be exact. Later, clarity of expression will become of first importance in this as in other arts. Thought, emotion, movement and speech which are vague and woolly are the bane of drama. The teacher should insist more and more on clear expression, though at the start he may have to do much of the clarification himself. ' Sort of ' and ' kind of ' and ' you know ' should be made to give place gradually to precise description.

Discussion of characters may not be fruitful at first. In stories appropriate to this age there is often little description of character, or only the simplest indications. But it will be profitable, even at the beginning, to encourage children to invest the characters they are to play with some imagined personality, however black and white. Their experience of people may be small, but it is often vivid. With some children, however, there may be a hiatus between the real world of personal experience and the imagined world of a dramatised story. Such a ' carry-over ' can be best effected, perhaps, by discussion. But early on they should begin to fill in for themselves the characters which they act; this will make the work more interesting to themselves and others. For example, ' What were Joan of Arc's father and mother like? Or Noah's children? Or Noah himself, besides being vaguely "good"'? It is important that children should observe sympathetically other people's personalities for many reasons, but for drama, obviously, it is fundamental. ' Oh, I know a man like Noah. He's a carpenter and he's got huge hairy arms, with "Polly" tattooed on one. The hairs on his arms are red. He's rather bald and got blue eyes and he smokes a little pipe which has always gone out. He preaches at our chapel in a squeaky voice for a long time in a high collar. He doesn't say much otherwise, and he watches every penny.' The teacher of intelligent children at the top of a Junior School might well be satisfied with such a contribution, elicited, perhaps by a series of questions. It should serve to bring Noah to life for many of the class.

The question ' Why? ' has particular value for clarifying ideas. ' Is the Prodigal Son actually going to leave home at the end of the first scene, or shall we end the scene when it is decided that he is to go away? ' ' Oh, have him actually leaving.' ' Why? ' Pause. ' Because it will look good, everyone waving and saying goodbye, icksetra.' ' Why will it look good? ' Pause. ' Everyone waving, icksetra.' Pause. ' Oh, and his mother might be crying and his father looking sad.' ' Why would they be sad? ' ' Because he's going away for a long time. . . . They may not ever see him again. . . . Like someone emigrating to Australia. . . . Or like a soldier going to the wars. . . . And I expect all the farm workers would be sad too, because they liked him.' ' Why did they like him? ' ' Oh, he was cheerful and made jokes and things.' ' Was the elder brother like that too? ' ' Oh no. He was serious, always working or thinking about the work.' The teacher who was lucky enough to elicit answers to his ' why's ' similar to the above would have added considerably to the content, emotional and otherwise, of this scene, and would have helped to build up the characters concerned. He would also have implanted the idea of an effective piece of (melodramatic—and why not at this age?) ' theatre '. He also, incidentally, ' fed ' ideas to the children and made them think constructively. And during the discussion serious argument may arise between two or more children, which may be as valuable for the listeners as for the disputants.

It is quite probable that the children may suggest a considerable variety of ideas, and the teacher will have to come to a decision, sooner rather than later, because of the pressure of time. But if there is sufficient time, he will be wise to try out two or three ideas to see which one works and to give the children the opportunity to decide between them. However, the inexperienced (and immature) teacher may find his own ideas hard to sacrifice. The children's ideas may seem tasteless, irrelevant, trite, but if they do not interfere with the dramatic unfolding of the story, he should accept them—at first, at any rate. Later in the development of the dramatisation of a story he might introduce improvements—mainly to set high standards.

If possible, the teacher should not dictate. He should allow the children the maximum of responsibility and initiative, which means that a majority vote will often decide. But the teacher must safeguard the will of the minority when he thinks that it is artistically more truthful, and there are moments when the children are ' off the beam ' or are not progressing sufficiently and the teacher must be prepared to lay down the law: after all, he is there to guide and to control, and children do not like to have it their own way all the time.

Obviously, the teacher must try to share out the chief parts and positions of responsibility with reasonable equality. But what about the children who do not want to act, or, like Bottom, want to play every part and direct as well? We all know the Bottoms. They cannot be allowed to ' steal the show ' all the time, and their egos may be gently deflated by giving them jobs of decreasing responsibility at appropriate moments. Complete and sudden deflation usually results in sulking or aggressive non-cooperation: it is less wasteful of time and temper to keep Bottom on our side. If we do not insist that children who do not wish to act should act, but watch, and if we encourage them to comment, they will quite often want to join in later when they see that it is enjoyable, and may discreetly be made to take part in a crowd scene, for instance, before they realise that they are doing so. They need to feel part of it all, however, and there are always connected jobs—continuity man, floor manager, prompter, director's secretary, tape machine expert, scene-shifter, props man, stage-manager—real or invented for them.

CHAPTER VI

Improvisation means, quite simply, making up a scene as you go along on a given idea or theme or situation. It is first cousin to charades and dumb crambo. It develops naturally out of the acted story, and at its best it can be one of the highest forms of creative drama, or, indeed, of children's creative work in any of the arts. It can be acted by groups of any size; it may contain dialogue, mime, movement, or dance-drama. We shall be concerned mainly with its most usual manifestation—several actors using dialogue and mime.

Improvisation may have several valuable results, besides those listed in an earlier chapter. When children in Junior Schools begin work on improvisations they are liable, after being given their subject, to stand with their heads very close together, every-one talking at once, for two minutes—and then act for half-an-hour, unless stopped. Or else they talk interminably, protest that they aren't ready when called upon to do their improvisation, and then act for two minutes. The first of these not over-exaggerated examples shows that ideas are probably lacking, that the children are revelling in their work, but they have little sense of shapeliness, selection, economy; in fact of construction. The second example may point to a glut of ideas, but a lack of concentration, of freedom of expression, of knowledge of how to combine ideas into an harmonious unity: or, very rarely, it may indicate a great sense of economy. In fact, improvisation should give increasing experience of craftsmanship and construction, bringing conscious consider-ation gradually to bear on (often) unconscious impulses to action. In short, ' think before you act '; but don't think for too long, or the result may be emotional and mental constipation, as in the second example above. To practise during lessons the precept ' think before you act ' may not be without its effect on future conduct; and the shaping of raw material to fit a given concept is a truly creative act. Dramatic construction is one of the most exacting exercises in original thought that children can experience in school, comparable in sheer difficulty with the writing of the sonnet or the short story. Over the course of time children will learn about contrast, climax, tension, dramatic irony, ' plugging ' necessary information, and other techniques of the playwright, as well as some techniques of the actor and the producer. An improvisation is a kind of cooperative spoken composition (in the school sense) and, though superficially easier for some, because not written, yet really harder to do well.

Improvisation is one of the main links binding dramatic work to the rest of the English syllabus, of which drama should form an integral part. (It is also, of course, always an art.) As stated above, this combined spoken composition, is a valuable form of expression for those children who find difficulty in putting ideas on paper, and a useful alternative for fluent writers. Any kind of original writing needs careful preparation. There can hardly be better preparation for creative writing than something in which the children have already been involved imaginatively, mentally and emotionally, and in which they may have been utterly absorbed. They should write well, especially in verse, upon such a matter, though after being brought to fruition in dramatic form an idea may not bear transplantation to any other medium. The teacher only can judge, and here again sensitivity is necessary. For example, children may write excellent ballads, about, say, Noah, after acting the story; or, after an improvisation, they may write good verse, especially free verse, on such a subject as ' ship-wreck ' or ' crashed in the jungle '; or good short stories after improvising ' the haunted house ' or ' the cliff top '. A short story read to the children might be followed by their improvisations of the story, and this followed by free verse versions. Or a ballad, spoken by some of the class and mimed by the rest, might be followed by improvisations of the ballad's story by groups of the children, and this followed by the story of the ballad written as a play. Or an improvisation might be written up in verse and a combined version used for choral speaking. Other examples will occur readily.

The various forms of drama provide fruitful preparation and subject-matter for many forms of original written and spoken expression. Communication of ideas, especially of those original to the author, and reception of ideas are the prime considerations of all English teaching. As preparation, source and medium of written work, drama has largely been ignored by teachers of English. Communication of their ideas by means of the spoken word occasionally reveals something more personal, truer and deeper than children will want to put on to paper, and for this reason may be more profitable than the conventional weekly composition. When acting in an improvisation the child may be far less guarded in expression, less inhibited in what (of himself) he is prepared to let others share. This more or less uninhibited expression of the self is good education, and may be good art. Our traditional fear of emotion and its (organised) expression in the class-room should give place to a more realistic attitude.

Improvisation, and other forms of creative drama, should improve the quality of children's spoken language, as well as their speech. Indeed, the two cannot be separated. Children will naturally speak spontaneously in their current idiom and in the accents of their neighbourhood. As regards any particular improvisation, this is of little account, provided their speech has vitality. It is immaterial, too, if everyone speaks simultaneously— as they often do. Later on, the necessity for making words clear to an audience will result from experience, and steps to improve audibility can be taken profitably then, when the incentive for improvement is there. If the story or theme on which children are working has fired their imaginations, its spirit may be reflected in the words which they use. If they are imaginatively quickened, the words, which they speak, however simple or slangy, may be heightened in intensity and take on a quality lacking in ordinary daily speech. In this case, those words may take on overtones for the children and never lose their emotional or imaginative aura. If, as with an acted story, the children have heard a story which is finely written and well read or told to them, the actual words of the story may have dug deep into them and may come out spontaneously in their improvisation. This sometimes happens with a story from the Bible or a legend, such as the Arthurian cycle, and children will speak, if not winged words, at any rate like young poets. This is one of the many reasons for avoiding trivial subject matter. In any lesson first-rate, appropriate subject matter is half the battle.

First-rate subject matter and imaginative infection by it may also benefit the way in which children speak. Fluency, clarity, incisiveness and pleasant sound, are likely to occur when a child has something definite and important to say and he is eager to say it. Spoken words which spring from intensity of feeling and are, so to speak, shining in the mind of the speaker as he says them are apt to come ringing from the mouth. If, in the course of their normal English lessons, children can acquire a relish for words, as intrinsically interesting things, they may also enjoy the sound of them in their own mouths as well as in their ears. Ear-training, then, is of value for English, as for other purposes. In the Primary School children can begin to become conscious of the sounds words make; and the more sensitive they are to words as such, the better they may tend to speak them. Many children are good mimics and they can begin to appreciate the different kinds of speech sounds and idiom obtaining in various parts of the country. They should be able to appreciate, to some extent, the different sounds, rhythm and idiom (in general, not in particular) of the speech of, for example, Scotland, Wales, Ireland, Cockney London, Yorkshire, Lancashire, the Midlands, Devon. By such constructive teaching and such experience their own personal speech and their powers of written and oral expression may be enriched.

Speech is a highly personal matter. An ugly voice and crude pronunciation may cause a deep feeling of inferiority. But consciousness of unfortunate speech does not usually arise till after the Primary School stage. Young children, mercifully, on hearing their own recorded voices can exclaim cheerfully, 'Cor! Don't we sound common!' Later, however, ugly speech can have the same unfortunate consequences as a physical defect. Slovenly, ineffectual speech should therefore be corrected earlier, so that children can speak a clear, vital regional speech in time to save themselves from unhappy self-consciousness. Some parents, who object to what they call 'posh' talk and whose snobbish attitude to speech improvement may do their children positive harm, greatly impede the efforts of schools. This relic of class-consciousness should go the way of other forms of class-consciousness. The best way to eradicate slovenly and unpleasant speech is to

provide opportunity and incentive for vigorous clarity of speech:
one such opportunity is improvisation.

An effective way to make children word- and sound-conscious
is to train them to listen. ' Children to-day never listen '; perhaps
they never did. Certainly, they will not listen unless they are
interested. They should be trained to listen carefully and to
record accurately what they have heard. In order to describe
with precision what they have heard they are likely to have
recourse to simile and metaphor, in fact, to associations of ideas.
They will need to think constructively; but they must first listen
accurately.

Another effective method for producing consciousness of
sound is to ask for sound impressions of places like railway
stations, air terminals, airports, markets, circuses, fairs, motor-
racing tracks, factories, football grounds. Such impressions can be
built up into sound ' poems ' with very definite rhythms, perhaps
accompanied by appropriate movements.

It is important that ' class-room drama ' should be firmly
linked with normal English work in the child's mind, as well as
in the school time-table (always remembering that performances
of plays by children are equally beneficial at the right stage of
maturity). Work in drama can arise out of, reinforce or supplement English studies. Need for dramatic expression may appear
at any moment, and not only in English lessons. Historical events
and situations often have dramatic potentialities. Some aspects of
human geography lend themselves to improvisation and may
contain elements of drama (for example, the colour problem). At
the conclusion of a Scripture lesson children might (and do) say,
' We could act that '. The above subjects, and others, are all
forms of English. Dramatic expression may tend to fix certain
kinds of information more firmly in the mind. Some poetry and
some fiction lend themselves to dramatic treatment. Parts of
English grammar can be taught in dramatic form. And the full
impact of dramatic literature can be obtained for most children
only when the text is brought to life in action. Special lessons
for drama, therefore, tend to frustrate some of the aims of both
drama and English.

In some schools lessons given wholly to drama are due to the presence on the staff of a drama specialist. Obviously, the Head will want as many classes as possible to have the benefit of this specialised knowledge, but it is a great asset when the drama specialist is also able to teach general English. But too often English and drama remain divorced from one another and both suffer, for neither can act as a fertilising agent to the other. Even when the drama specialist is wholly engaged in his own subject, he should maintain a close and lively liason with the English staff—and they should welcome this.

Specialist knowledge, though clearly desirable, is not necessary for the achievement of effective work in drama. Given an interest in drama, some knowledge of contemporary ideas on the teaching of drama, and the normal qualities which go to make a good teacher, those who wish can do admirable work—and many do. Knowledge of theatre techniques is unnecessary and, indeed, may sometimes be harmful when there is the temptation to think of children's work too early in terms of theatrical proficiency.

If it is desirable that children should begin to realise the fundamental unity of various branches of learning (English and drama, for instance), it is also valuable that they should begin to appreciate that one idea can be expressed in different ways and in different media. A child's life tends to be artificially compartmentalized: home and school: term and holidays; lessons and play; English, poetry, reading, drama; history, geography, scripture; breakfast, dinner, tea. He tends to regard these compartments as separate ways of living with little carry-over from one to the other, though the rhythm and regularity with which they follow each other may tend to give him security. Yet the sooner he can begin to realise (even unconsciously) the essential unity of life, the better; and the practice of the arts can begin to show him the way. Further, by beginning to understand simple relationships, such as those between the main facts of daily living, he may be led to see relationships and associations between ideas which are not obviously related, and this is the start of constructive thought.

Improvisation provides opportunity for the exercise of this faculty of seeing relationships. From their conglomeration of assorted memories, personal and vicarious, hitherto unrelated factors may be knit together in the minds of the group to make a

D

new entity. One child's memory of a hidden treasure story might fuse with another's recollection of an ornate fireplace, seen in a mansion ' open to the public ', to form the dénouement of a scene about the discovery of hidden treasure behind a fireplace in an empty house. Or a ghost story might be linked to the memory of a lonely house on a moor seen during a summer holiday. Such fusion of ideas is not unlike inspiration.

But this reorganisation of previous ideas has to be made explicit in action. It must be made intelligible to those taking part and to anyone who is watching. This means clear thinking and clear expression in speech and action. We learn to think by prac- tising thinking, and one of the best ways to practise thinking is to make plans about something which interests us; and one of the most interesting kinds of plan to make is a plan for future (imagin- ative) action. An improvised scene will necessitate thinking about practical considerations, as well as about imaginative ones—what exactly we are going to do and say and how precisely we are going to do it and say it. And, having planned, we have to carry our plan into effect, with clarity. To do this convincingly we have to keep on thinking, making up speech and action to suit the general plan, and carry that general plan forward to its definitive end, with clarity. An admirable exercise in thinking—and one that is fun and all ' our own '.

Improvisation entails another form of thought—that of critical thinking. It is often customary at the end of an improvisation for the teacher to criticise the work and to invite comment from the rest of the class. It is also unusual for a class of children in a Junior School to produce any worthwhile criticism. Beyond an occasional remark, such as ' I couldn't hear what Rosemary said ', they generally have little to offer. This is hardly surprising as their experience of dramatic work may be slender and their critical faculties are largely undeveloped. Nevertheless, this opportunity for criticism is valuable. A child's comment may provoke dis- agreement and discussion, or an opportunity for the teacher use- fully to digress. But much value can emerge, if criticism and discussion is led by the teacher. For example,

' It wasn't clear to me that they were looking for hidden treasure. They just came in and started hunting around. Was it clear to you? '

' Yes.'

' Is that because you know now? '

' Yes—I suppose it is really.'

' How could they have made it clear to us that they were looking for hidden treasure? '

' One might have said, " I wonder where that treasure can be".'

' Yes. Any other suggestions? '

' One of them might have had a plan showing where the treasure was hidden and they could have talked about it.'

' Yes. That would have been a natural thing for them to do and it would have told us what they were looking for. Another thing. I thought the scene rather fizzled out. They didn't seem very excited when they'd dug the treasure up, and nothing much seemed to happen afterwards. How could they have improved the ending? '

' They might have talked about what they would do with the treasure. How they were going to spend the money, icksetra.'

' Yes. Not very dramatic, though.'

' They might have started quarrelling over their shares.'

' Yes. That's much more dramatic. Quarrels are always dramatic.'

' One of them might have got killed during the quarrel.'

' Good! But they'd have to work out exactly why and how he was killed. Any more ideas? '

' Well, when they'd dug up the treasure and opened the box, they might have found it was empty.'

' I'm not sure that's not the best idea of the lot. A complete surprise for us all. Surprise, too, is dramatic. . . .'

Then, with these new ideas the group could go to work again on their improvisation.

If carefully guided, constructive criticism and consequent discussion may teach children much about drama, act as an example of critical thinking, gradually induce a critical attitude to their own work, as well as that of others, and become another forum in which children are able to discuss specific ideas. The objectively criticial attitude will be slow in developing, and none the worse for that: but its seeds may be planted in the Junior School.

Improvisation entails the assumption of almost complete

responsibility by a group of children for the combined creation of a work of art. Given a subject for their scenes, they have to decide the rest—plot, perhaps, characters, dialogue, situations. One or more of the group may assume the leadership, but all can make suggestions. Apart from their work in the art room, this is, may be, the sole official occasion during the school week on which they are called upon to bear such responsibility. It is responsibility which is fun to exercise and brings a real and legitimate sense of power and achievement, and does not weigh heavily on their shoulders. To have a share in the responsibility for the joint creation of something new is a form of positive, constructive responsibility, and the ' officialness ' of this form of collective responsibility gives the same kind of *cachet* as group responsibility for independent work on a class ' project '. We spend much of our lives in coming to decisions. Children can scarcely have too much practice in making up their minds, particularly when, as in this case, their decisions will be concerned with affairs of the imagination and not of real life; when the results of the decisions can be seen immediately, and the effects of the causes are at once apparent; when the making of the decisions need not involve the emotions and can be objectively and dispassionately sought. The handing out of appropriate responsibility is one of the chief ways of promoting maturity.

Improvisation can be such a valuable and rewarding experience for children in the Junior or Secondary School that it has seemed worth while to consider its potentialities at some length. At any rate, improvisation should be taken very seriously by its exponents; and by those who maintain that drama in school is a ' frill ' or a ' soft option '.

It remains to make some suggestions about the actual practice of improvisation.

Space. The acting area should be reasonably large, if possible, but not too big; this is not a movement class, small groups may suffer from agoraphobia—besides, improvisation is an intimate affair. After all, a gang of children play many of their games in a confined space, even out of doors. It is not a bad training to have to economise movements to fit in with the available space. Gradual restriction of acting area, from the wide spaces of the hall to the four walls (and desks) of the class-room, will reflect the increasing skill and homogeneity of children's work. Too much space at this stage may lead to loose, unorganised movements, loose chaotic dialogue, lack of tautness of plot; a smaller space may induce more closely-knit work. Proximity of the actors to one another should lead to increased sensitivity of playing: they should be able to watch each other's eyes. Of course, the ideal size of the ' set ' will depend on the nature of each particular improvisation.

Numbers. The number of children in each group will obvious-ly depend on the subject of the improvisation. Some subjects will need large numbers in each group; but such subjects should be avoided, in general, for the fewer the children, the more will have the chance to play important parts. Six or eight are useful numbers to have in the groups; particularly, perhaps, eight, for 5 x 8 = 40, which is a usual size for a class, particularly in Primary Schools (where, of course, it ought to be half this number). This gives five groups which is a workable number and allows, perhaps, five minutes per improvisation.

Timing. Timing is most important and undeniably difficult to organise: so much has to be crammed into a small space of time. The subject or subjects for improvisation have to be announced. Some discussion and ' feeding ' of ideas must take place, in the initial stage of this work, at any rate. If all the groups are improvising the same or similar subjects, some preliminary movement may be advisable. There may be questions. The groups must have time to discuss and rehearse their scenes as fully as possible. Each group has to act their improvisation, with comment and criticism afterwards. Finally, the teacher should have time for general comments. All this usually has to take place during one lesson, probably of 40 minutes. Often, the next drama period will be in a week's time. If this is the case, it may be a mistake to carry over the work till the following week. So much will have happened in the children's lives during that week, the initial impetus and excitement will have vanished, and they will have to start again almost from scratch. But if the drama is taken by a teacher of English as an integral part of the English work, then there is not so much pressure, and the improvisations can be carried over to the next English lesson, which is probably the next day. Even this, however, is much less satisfactory than completing the whole thing in one continuous period of time. So strict timing becomes necessary—definite time limits, which are not to be exceeded, for preparing and for acting improvisations. It may be possible to announce the subjects of the improvisations a day or so beforehand, so that the children are able to do some preliminary planning, which may save time. But the original fire and interest is liable to fade whenever there is a gap of time between conception and execution.

How should the subject matter of improvisations develop over the course of time? As has been suggested already, improvisations should grow gradually out of the ' acted story '. Progress in the demands made by improvisations should match the degree of the children's maturity. Improvisations should become increasingly exacting, and the sensitive teacher will know when the children are ready for another push forward. He will probably judge from the degree of absorption of the children in the current improvisations. When ready to move forward they will become unsatisfied and concentration will tend to fade early.

Many teachers are apt to start improvisations at the wrong end, with realism. They reason that children will improvise best on that which is most familiar to them, so they give subjects such as ' Father wins the pools ', ' hanging out the washing ', ' the family at breakfast '. Real life is one of the hardest things to portray convincingly. It needs the dramatist with the ' seeing eye ' and the actor of assured technique to make it true and living. It must be more real than reality, larger than life, and full of imaginative insight. Or it must abound in the humour that comes from experience and sympathetic observation of character. These are difficult achievements for young children. Realism should come at the end of a course of improvisation. At the beginning should come the romantic, to match the children's essentially romantic stage of life—for example, the Sacrifice of Isaac; Elisha and the Shulamite; incidents from the Song of Roland, Beowulf, or Hiawatha, and so on. The Bible, myth, legend, history are as full of plots for improvisations as they are of stories for acting.

The first purely group improvisations might centre round what may be called sensational subjects—headline stuff. ' Street Accident ', ' Mine Disaster ', ' Shipwreck '. (' Mine Disaster ' is usually a winner). Such subjects are non-realistic in an important sense, in that they need not demand close observation of character or first-hand experience of life to make them convincing to the participants; they can be treated ' romantically '. These scenes may need large casts, and may be expressed in movement and mime, which are no great disadvantages at this early stage, for the children will be on familiar ground. Such subjects will probably need a certain amount of direction by the teacher— again, probably advantageous at this stage. They will make no great demands on the children. But they may not necessarily be dramatic in the real sense of the word, and children should gain a sense of what is truly dramatic reasonably soon: improvisation should be dramatic, not merely sensational. If there is to be little or no speech, it may be helpful to use sound effects, probably those which the children can make themselves at the time, or which they have recorded on tape. This first stage is a recapitulation, a *reculer pour mieux sauter*. It should not last too long and, indeed, may be dispensed with altogether with promising children.

Next might come plots; plots of suitable existing plays, or plots of stories which have dramatic possibilities. But what is dramatic? A pageant is not in itself dramatic, though it may contain dramatic scenes; nor are some stories, from history or elsewhere. For example, the stories of Florence Nightingale, Robert Clive and Lawrence of Arabia are not themselves neces- sarily dramatic, though they contain dramatic moments. The same is true of a documentary film or play or radio sequence, though they may contain drama. For the present writer—and with no apologies whatever to certain modern playwrights—the old answer is the most satisfactory. Conflict. Opposition. Tension. Tension, leading to comic or sad or tragic ends, between men; or between creatures or beings endowed with human qualities; or between ideas symbolised in a man, and other men; or conflict within an individual. The tension, its development and resolution must arise as the result of the ideas, emotions and actions of characters in the play. Man is at the centre of drama. For example, 'Anti-

gone ' (which should be preceded by some explanation to children
of Greek ideas about burial) contains, among others, these dramatic
situations and ideas—the horror of the sorrowing sisters, Antigone
and Ismene, at their uncle Creon's refusal to bury the body of
their brother Polynices, while the brother whom he slew and by
whom he was slain, Eteocles, has been given burial; Antigone's
decision to disobey Creon's order that Polynices may not be
buried, and thereby to risk death; the conflicting points of view
on this matter of Ismene and Antigone, and the contrasted characters of the two sisters; the complication of Antigone's betrothal
to Haemon, Creon's son; Antigone's seizure in the act of trying to
bury Polynices; her defiance of Creon; the struggle in Creon over
the implementation of his law and the condemnation of his niece
and his son's betrothed; Antigone condemned to death; the deaths
of Antigone, Haemon and Eurydice, Creon's wife; the agony and
repentance of Creon. The plot (and the play) are packed with
drama.

Tension, the balance of opposing forces, is a condition of our
life and of our art, whether we are composing a picture or a play,
or taking part in a class-room discussion, or just existing. It is
good that children should see tension objectively (if unconsciously)
functioning in imagined situations which are more or less relevant
to life as they know it.

Plots of plays in simple outline will provide plenty of material
for improvisations in one or more scenes. ' Julius Caesar ',
' Macbeth ', ' Coriolanus '. Some of Molière, shortened and
abridged—' Le Médecin malgré lui ', ' Le Malade Imaginaire '.
Some of Shaw—' The Devil's Disciple ', 'Androcles and the
Lion '. Synge's ' Riders to the Sea ', perhaps ' The Playboy of
the Western World '. Drinkwater's 'Abraham Lincoln ', ' Oliver
Cromwell '. ' Cyrano de Bergerac ', ' The Scarlet Pimpernel ',
' The Bells ', ' The Lyons Mail ', ' The Prisoner of Zenda ',
' Berkeley Square ', Lord Dunsany's 'A Night at an Inn '. These
are a few random suggestions. At first, each group might improvise
the whole of a plot, but at a later stage the division of the plots
into scenes could be discussed by the class, each group be given
a different scene, and all the scenes be played consecutively
after each separate scene has been acted and criticised. This

may necessitate alternations to individual scenes so that the whole may be consistent and unified, which will give valuable experience of the principle of unity.

For stories with dramatic plots teachers may find omnibus volumes of short stories useful, as well as, for example, the Sherlock Holmes stories, the Father Brown stories, some Kipling stories, some of the more respectable stories of French writers (Mérimée's 'Mateo Falcone', the de Maupassant stories of the Franco-Prussian war). Occasionally a story should be read in full in order to inspire and give ideas, but usually at this stage the plot can be summarized in a few sentences. But not all stories which contain episodes are necessarily suitable for acting.

Other plots with dramatic potentialities come to mind—the hatred and fear of the challenging and therefore unpopular personality (e.g. Galileo); the hunting, trial and death of a witch: the betrayal of a plot to commit murder, to revolt; the person who will not sacrifice his principles; the discovery and capture of a spy; the last moment pardon; and so on. After improvising plots of this nature children may begin to have some instinctive idea of what is dramatic. At this stage criticism might focus on the lack of the dramatic, and in discussion children might be guided towards a definition of the dramatic.

The next series of improvisations should be centred on the basic stuff of drama, human character. A useful introduction to this series would be some discussion of actual personalities (not connected with the school) known to invididual children. Such discussion could be initiated, perhaps, by individual oral descriptions followed by questioning, or by short written descriptions read aloud. Perhaps the children might also be asked to reproduce the speech, the movements and other characteristics of the personalities they are describing. This has its dangers, for some children may be tempted to try for a cheap laugh (there are usually one or two would-be comics), and when improvising may mimic instead of imagining and thinking sincerely. But, certainly, children should be reminded that everyone's speech and movements are uniquely their own and that mere imitation and portrayal of 'types' is facile, superficial and unworthy, and may be cruel. Indeed, these improvisations (and all others too) could profitably be preceded by relevant movement experience. In addition to general discussion of personalities, there could with profit be some preliminary discussion of the particular characters which are about to be improvised, especially if the same subject is given to each group; not only how this or that person will move or speak, but how he or she is likely to feel and think in the given circumstances of the improvisation, and what, in consequence, he or she is likely to do and say. Such actions should be ' rehearsed ' by everyone. At a later stage in this series children should be reminded of the great importance of making the plot of their improvisation grow out of the actions, thought and feelings of the characters.

Suggestions for subjects for improvisations on character are— the magician, the tyrant, the importunate invalid, the ballet-dancer, the helpful ghost, the inefficient shop-assistant, the cowardly burglar, the ineffectual spy, the zealous policeman, the kindly giant, the outlaw, the highwayman, the poacher, the tramp, the nightwatchman, the hospital matron. But—and it is a big but— these suggested characters, and others of a similar kind, may lead to ' type-acting '. It is essential that such characters should be woven into a dramatic plot, or they may never come to real life and remain a bit of artificial ' play-acting '. There are also the characters of history, of the Bible, of legend. At first, a good many suggestions of characteristics for the characters and of ideas for plots may be necessary, but later the children should be left more and more to their own devices, until they are able to improvise with confidence from a straight-forward title. The teacher should look for rounded, convincing, simple characterisation in speech, movement and words, as well as dramatic tension, whether humorous or serious. Improvisation around characters will tend to be realistic, of everyday life; the teacher must be wary of possible slickness, lack of imaginative thought and insincerity.

A harder series of subjects might follow next; subjects which make demands on the ingenuity and initiative of the children, subjects which are just starting-points, give little direct help, but some indirect suggestion, and which may or may not quickly fire their imaginations. The children may feel bewildered by these subjects at first, but as they start to think about them and work on them, the imagination usually lights up. The first of these 'springboard' series may be called 'Props'. Objects. A telephone, a telegram, a letter, a knife, a book, a chair, a clock, a tape-recorder. Any object. The combined ingenuity of a group will usually be able to weave a plot round an object, though at first they may need some hints. For example—

'You're stuck over "the chair"'? Well, what position might the chair be in?'
'Standing up, I suppose.'
'Yes.'
'Lying on its side.'
'What could have caused it to lie on its side?'
'A fight.'
'What caused the fight?'
'Someone came in and found a burglar in the room.'
And they're off.

The need to make the object central to the improvisation should not inhibit dramatic tension or convincing characterisation.

The next of this series which is rather similar to the 'Props' improvisations, might be called 'Locations'. The door, the window, the cliff top, in the train, the native village, the tower, the prison cell, the jungle clearing, the cave. What can be done with a door (real or imagined), for example? A ghost, a thief, a policeman, a gangster, your long-lost sister, a telegraph boy can come in; the prisoner, the condemned man, the loser in a quarrel, the furious parent can go out.

The third of this 'springboard' series might be called 'Lines'; to start children off on an improvisation by giving the first or the last line of a scene or scenes.

'So it was you, was it?'
'Take him away, Constable.'
'You come too late.'
'Saved!'
(Last lines).
'What are you doing here?'

' Idiot! You might have shot me! '
' Now, listen carefully. This is the plan: . . .'
' For heaven's sake, stop crying now! '
(First lines).

Combinations of these ' springboard ' subjects are also possible.
In all of them the children will need to be imaginative, resourceful
and self-reliant.

By this time it ought to be possible to take for granted that the
children are striving after the dramatic and after convincing characterisation in all their improvisations. To these fundamental
qualities, that of simple, suitable construction might now be added.
For example, each scene should contain a climax, or a series of
climaxes rising in crescendo to a main climax. If their previous
improvisations have been truly dramatic, it is likely that the
children, quite unconsciously, have already included climaxes in
their scenes. They might now be made conscious of this fact.

' In your improvisations one group made the owners of a
flat come in late at night to discover two masked thieves. One
thief was laid out cold, the other was bound to the chair. When
this thief's mask was removed, the owner recognised his brother
who had always hated him, and now had come to rob him out of
jealousy and revenge. This sudden discovery of the brother was
the main climax of the scene. . . .'

It is important to make sure that in the preparation of their
improvisations the children think first of a dramatic plot and
secondly of its climaxes—first the imaginative impulse, perhaps
the inspiration, and the main ideas; then the craft and craftsmanship of expressing those ideas. The technicalities of the making of
plays must be approached carefully and not too prematurely, or
sincerity and spontaneity may vanish.

Perhaps at this stage another principle of construction might
be considered—that of the effective ending—surprise, reconciliation, justice done, and so on. The tension is resolved, or a new
problem, not to be solved, is stated. (The latter is perhaps over-
subtle).

These ' springboard ' improvisations have tended towards the
realistic, and with their greater experience, the insistent emphasis
on the dramatic, on convincing characterisation, and now on

construction, children could begin at this stage to improvise scenes in which realism is paramount. They should be sufficiently experienced by now not to fall into the trap of triviality and facetiousness, such as ' the family row ', ' at the seaside ', ' the rainy day ', ' shopping ', ' washing day ' often produce.

The last of this list of subjects and much the most difficult concerns mood or emotion. Anger, fear, jealousy, forgiveness, hope, grief, generosity. These abstract emotions, as such, should not be given to children as subjects for improvisation, but subjects should be given them which have an obvious underlying emotion, such as ' Two of the men are missing '. Here, a family might receive news that father and son are involved in, for example, a mine disaster and display grief and anxiety. Such scenes have a clear climax which is a great virtue. It is of little use to attempt to act, for example, ' anger '; but one can act a person who is angry in a real situation. The expression of the emotion must come from within, if it is to be convincing. A few suggestions are—escape from threatened danger, persuasion to do something uncongenial, reconciliation, dissuasion from a dangerous course of action; also ' the Strike ', ' at the Dentist's ', ' Betrayed ', ' the Parting ', ' the Wedding ', ' the Last Hope ', ' the Will '. Preparatory work in movement will be useful here, partly in order to ' set ' the mood. These moods and emotions are often difficult for children to sustain for the full length of an improvisation and success will depend largely on the amount of imaginative concentration. Clearly, the moods must be within the experience of children. Some teachers have a way of springing upon children improvisation exercises concerned with mood. ' Be frightened,' they will say to a class, ' be sad, be joyful '. The children have not been prepared, they are not caught up in any imaginary situation, nor identified with any specific character. They will react with some cliché action; the results will be false and superficial.

Towards the end of the work on improvisation the children should learn two more ideas about play construction. In previous work they will probably have encountered dramatic irony (the audience knows something which the characters in the play do not). They should now be brought to realise its dramatic possibilities. ' In your improvisation on " The Wedding ", we knew that the bridegroom had started for Australia, but the characters in the scene didn't.' Further plots containing dramatic irony might be suggested for them to work out. And there is the all-important factor of unity. Scenes must hang together, be one. There must be no cheating, as in some detective stories, where a new character, guilty of the crime, is introduced at the last moment. Tension should have arisen from known circumstances, from the main characters and be resolved by them. There should be no inconsistency nor too many loose ends. The whole thing should be tidy, taut, shapely, convincing.

A useful variation is to set different subjects concerned with the same main idea to different groups. A simple example is—the aircrew's room, the customs, the security officer's room, the control room, the passengers' lounge; all centred round an airport and perhaps generically called, ' Tragedy at the airport ', or ' Crime at an airport '. Here is a chance for the children to contrast different characters concerned with the same event, the ways in which they speak and move, what they say, how they feel and show their feelings. At the end the improvisations could be fitted together to make a ' documentary '.

Solo improvisations are definitely not for children: they are for older adolescents and adults.

Work on any one improvisation may continue for just as long as the children are interested—and no longer. As soon as they begin to tire of it, it is time to scrap it ruthlessly and go on to something new. When they show signs of boredom it is often an indication that they have grown out of that particular stage of the work and need (but not necessarily desire) to progress onward to something more exacting.

On the other hand some improvisations will give particular satisfaction. The teacher will know when this occurs because the children will be especially absorbed in it and because he himself will probably be moved as he watches. Two courses of action are then open to him. He can leave it there, as an expression of truth, a real achievement, though perhaps not technically perfect, and introduce something completely new; or he and the children can go to work on it, polishing it up. He will know which to do by direct questioning and by the demands of the children. ' Oh, please, can't we go on with it? ' If he decides to continue working on it, he must be prepared to find that its first bloom vanishes, that the original appears distressingly humdrum, that they have to do a great deal of hard work on it before it begins to approach excellence once more, and that in the end they have made something very different from the first version. Nevertheless, this is all good experience for the children, particularly the need for perseverance when their work appears to be falling to bits in their hands. Before they start ' polishing ' the teacher must give them (through guided discussion) very clear ideas about the main improvements necessary, and he must help them continuously with encouraging, precise and constructive comment—and he must make them go through with it to the end. When it is satisfactorily completed the children, if still interested, might each write the improvisation in play form. There will then be several differing variations of the same play script: an agreed script can be constructed, and there is a group play which has already stood the test of successful production. This script can be put to further use, as will appear later; for the moment it is the concrete evidence of fruitful enterprise.

Improvisation is perhaps the most valuable of all the various forms of creative drama in schools. It becomes in its later stages, when the children have complete responsibility for it, a form of truly cooperative creation, calling for everything—physically, mentally, emotionally—that the participants can give. It embraces all the main facets of dramatic enterprise, those of playwright, actor, producer and perhaps designer. It is not just a weekly bit of fun. It should be fun, but it will be far greater fun, if it becomes progressively more exacting, more skilled, more ambitious, more mature. The last stages of improvisation are the mid-point of a progressive course of dramatic work which lasts throughout the school career of a boy or girl. Without a full experience of improvisation later work with scripts may prove profoundly disappointing.

There remain other useful dramatic and semi-dramatic activities which are appropriate to this stage—that is the top of the Junior School and the lower half of the Secondary School.

The 'Documentary'. There are very many possible subjects. A class might be making a local survey in history lessons. The results of their investigations might issue in the form of a pageant of scenes (dramatic or not) from the history of the locality, written, produced, acted, and if possible designed, by the children. Here are history, English, particularly in its dramatic aspect, and perhaps art and craft integrated in a single creative enterprise. An English class might make a documentary out of scenes from the book or narrative poems or ballads they have read, each child having the opportunity to dramatise these scenes, to act in one or more of them, and assist actively in their production. Or the documentary might have a sociological connection; a favourite in girls' schools (or colleges) is the Emancipation of Women. Or the term's Scripture lessons might form the subject of a documentary. Documentaries give scope for originality, enterprise, imaginative reconstruction, creative ability, the relating of school subjects to real life, and they provide plenty of responsible jobs for everybody, not least those who do not care for acting.

Films. One Junior School class which was making a study of the local church and its surroundings completed a film of the whole proceeding. When the study was finished the class set up an exhibition (writings, drawings, paintings, rubbings, specimens), invited the parents, gave them lectures on their own church, showed them the film, gave them tea and charged them a shilling or so to help pay for the film. This was a magnificent educational enterprise, though not really drama. Other schools have made films of school events and the school life. These are not dramatic pursuits, of course, but they point the way. Some schools have, in fact, made films of a more dramatic nature. But someone has to have the money to spare.

Filming and Television techniques. These may provide useful incentives and aids to improvisations, or acted stories, particularly for classes of apathetic children. It will be a useful exercise in written English to turn a plot or a story into a rough film 'treatment'. It will probably be interesting to turn the treatment into shooting sequences. It may be of less interest to pretend to shoot them (unless you are lucky enough to have a real film camera).

The acting of the sequences may be a valuable alternative to improvisation, while the various officials of the film studio will provide jobs for those who are not particularly keen to act, and the 'let's pretend' of the film studio or location may provide a thrill for the ingenuous and under-sophisticated. The TV technique is more akin to stage drama and provides almost as many studio jobs for the non-actors,—camera-men, boom-man, lighting, sound effects, props, etc.—with one post of great responsibility for the floor manager, who has to organize the studio so that all the actors and equipment do not get in each other's way and everything works smoothly. In both cases the working out of the various kinds of shots and the grouping (especially with TV) of characters can provide opportunity for ingenuity and the eye of the artist. Here, with imaginary viewers in mind, there can be a first beginning of insistence on the visibility and audibility of the actors.

Sound broadcasting techniques—the radio play (the scripting of which will be another valuable English exercise). The school with microphones (real or sham) and a Tannoy system have an advantage here, obviously, but use can be made of tape machine microphones also. Younger children will have little difficulty in ' pretending ' the equipment. Being a non-visual medium, depending entirely on the voice to create illusion, this may prove a difficult technique for them, though shyer children may come sometimes to enjoy and profit from being heard but not necessarily seen. It may be better postponed until children are more mature and have more control of their voices. For speech work it can be a very useful medium. The choice of material will need care. It may be better to try for broader dramatic effects, the simple and, perhaps, melodramatic, remembering that children are unlikely to be able to convey with their voices alone subtleties of character or tension. Sound effects may be important and should be as realistic as possible; by their very realism they will give an impetus to the actors and to the scene. It will be worth while (as well as fun) to get exact recordings on tape. The whole scene or improvisation might profitably be tape-recorded, so that it can be played back and necessary alterations made later. Children always enjoy hearing their own voices, particularly on tape, and they may

E

realise that their voices and speech could be improved. This recording of children's original work is one of the really profitable uses to which the tape machine can be put. Besides sound effects, the children might also experiment with *musique concrète*, both for its own sake and for use in dramatic work.

There has been interesting pioneer work, particularly in Birmingham, in the use of stage lighting, by which children have been enabled to paint, as it were, with lights upon an open playing-space in pursuance of their dramatic aims. Not everybody will have the equipment or the courage to allow children to do this. It must be extraordinarily satisfying to be able to experiment with lighting, either for particular sets, or just for the sheer fun of it. Perhaps for sensible and efficient children reasonably effective and cheap lighting apparatus could be rigged up with batteries, flex, bulbs, biscuit tins and a few gellies. Most children would enjoy and profit from playing around with such equipment—and so would many of their teachers—but the risks may be considerable.

There are also exercises of various kinds which may prove useful when children are mature enough for realism—for example, telephone conversations and interviews (press, radio, television). If treated as dramatic scenes in themselves, they need as careful preparation and discussion by teacher and children as any other form of dramatic work; if they are preliminary exercises for an improvisation, they will have sufficient purpose and imaginative background to ensure probable concentration and satisfaction. Without such aids to absorption and sincerity these exercises are liable to become trivial and as great a waste of time as the ' be sad ', ' be frightened ' type of exercise. But if the children are absorbed in the exercise, it may be particularly valuable for expression of character by voice without much help from physical movement. Children can rehearse these exercises in pairs or small groups simultaneously, and comment on each other's work after ' performance '.

The term ' Dance-Drama ' has different meanings for different people. For many dance-drama is the expression of a theme or idea (dramatic or otherwise) in terms of dance, or dance and dramatic movement, with or without music or percussion. As such, it is an art-form in its own right, but usually more akin to dance than drama. This form of dance-drama, therefore, will not be discussed here, except to say that in some schools, particularly girls' schools, and in women's training colleges work of real quality in this genre sometimes takes place.

In some schools dance-drama takes another form. Children listen to a piece of music and then decide how the ideas and emotions within the music itself, or the emotions evoked by the music, or both, can be expressed in terms of dance or mime or drama, or a combination of these. The music is not necessarily programme music; indeed, it is probably better not programme music, for this may inhibit the flow of free ideas by its representational qualities and the resulting dance-drama may become partly imitative. The choice of music is obviously of prime importance. If some programme music is to be excluded, it will not always be easy to find music which evokes dramatic ideas. Music—most abstract of all arts—which evokes dance ideas will be comparatively easy to discover. And the music should be likely to communicate dramatic ideas to the whole group, for one of the merits of dance-drama is that responsibility for the outcome lies with the children, each of whom may have a different interpretation, and discussion, therefore, may be fiercely contested.

Apart from the difficulty of choosing suitable music, this form of dance-drama has its dangers, as well as its values. By definition, the action, of whatever kind, will be accompanied by music, which may lead to sentimentality, or emotional wallowing, or insincerity —to falsity, in fact. And the children may learn to lean too heavily on music as an aid to the free expression of ideas or emotions— an especial danger—when they turn to spoken drama. Dance-drama, too, may tend towards the expression of movement or dance ideas solely; or it may become mime done to music; in fact it may ignore the spoken word completely. Drama depends largely on character; it is difficult to express character in terms of the body only. The drama part of dance-drama may vanish. The children probably enjoy it thoroughly, but they may become bogged down in it to the exclusion of normal progress in drama. It is dangerous to be stuck at a certain stage in anything. It is seldom completely satisfactory to interpret a work of art in terms

of another art-form—particularly, perhaps, two such different
arts as music and drama. In short, this form of dance-drama is a
stage, and a valuable one.

But it calls for a most exacting effect of the imagination. To
have to ' see ' story and resulting action in a piece of music, and
then translate this into dance and movement and, perhaps, speech
which are appropriate both to the music and to the invented story
requires something of the order of vision. That children can and
do effect this should be a salutary shock to those who under-
estimate the capabilities of children—and it is not necessarily the
more intelligent children who excel in dance-drama. Dance-
drama may incidentally give a deeper insight into music. A good
deal of experience and practice of movement is necessary, if work in
dance-drama is to be satisfying. This is all to the good, and a
strong idea as a basis for movement may give it greater significance
for the mover and so enable him to communicate more to the
others working with him.

In strictly literal terms, ' West Side Story ', without most of
the lyrics and all the dialogue, in other words with its music and,
above all, its dance is a magnificent example of dance-drama.
(For those who have not seen it, ' West Side Story ' is ' Romeo
and Juliet ' in up-to-the-minute New York idiom).

Perhaps the conception of this kind of dance-drama should be
inverted; first, the central idea (e.g. the ' Romeo and Juliet '
story); then, the working out of the scenario, the action and the
movements to express these; and, lastly, the choice of suitable
music. As it stands, the interpretation of music in terms of action
is a valuable experience at the appropriate stage in a course of
drama, and at most stages an admirable variation on normal work.

It must be emphasized that dance-drama has nothing to do
with the normal teaching of music and should in no way militate
against this.

CHAPTER VII

Children should not attempt to act a play written by an adult (a printed play) until they are ready for it; until, that is, they are sufficiently mature and reasonably experienced in the kind of work outlined above. They should be able to bring some understanding of human character to the interpretation of the characters in the play. In reading a play text they should be able to recognise human qualities which have come within their experience, such as warm-heartedness, ill-temper, generosity, fussiness, though they may not always be able to supply the appropriate descriptive word (to have to do so may enrich their active vocabulary). From this simple knowledge of human beings they should be able to say whether or not the actions and the remarks of the characters in a play ring true. They may not yet be skilled enough to convey by their acting the truth of a character, as they see it, but that does not matter; even though they cannot yet act the character well, they should have ideas about how it might be done. They should have some appreciation of the dramatic qualities of the play, and many will be able to visualize how a given situation will appear in action. For example, they might say, ' Phew, it'll be super when they come in with the reprieve, as he's standing with the noose round his neck! '

' Well, how shall we do it? '

' He'll be up on a rostrum in the middle, with the hangman one side and the clergyman on the other, and all the people will be standing round, and the soldiers will come rushing in from over there, pushing through the crowd and shouting.'

' Let's try it out, then.'

They should be able to speak and to move with confidence and decision, and be able to say what they mean in improvisation—however simply—with voice and body. They should be able to relax. They should have a degree of self-discipline, and be able to obey orders promptly from the producer, whether a teacher or, more usually, one of themselves. They should be able to see the play as a whole and not merely their own part in it.

These are mature qualities and children should have acquired them, to some extent, through their previous experience in dramatic work and in life, before they begin to act a play text. Without these qualities and without this previous experience, attempts to act a text may be far less effective, less convincing, less true and less genuinely satisfying to the actors and to the teacher.

The transition from improvisation to scripted play needs tactful and delicate handling, for it is the transition from creation to creation-interpretation.

The argument as to where true creation lies in the production of a play is ancient and undetermined. Actors, producers and designers are concerned, individually and collectively, with the search for and expression of the truth of a play text. It is arguable that the only real creator is the author. That may be so; what matters in schools is that the utmost freedom should be given to the expression of the truth of a play as the children see it. It may not be the author's truth, or the teacher's, but no two people will probably agree fully about the truth of any work of art. With children the realisation in action of the truth of a play text, as they see it, may well be as fully creative as their realisation in action of a story which has been told or read to them.

One danger of the transition from creation to creation-interpretation is the attitude of some teachers who say, in effect, ' We've finished with all that childish stuff and now we can get on with the real thing' . ' The childish stuff ' is very much ' the real thing ' at any age (stage students learn through improvisation: some productions of both professional plays and films lean heavily on improvisation) and as will appear, improvisation is a useful tool in the production of a play. Teachers with this attitude of mind may be self-indulgent, combine a love of theatre with a love of power, and so be tempted to over-direct children's work on a play-text. And the worst of it is that the children may agree with the teacher in thinking, ' now at last we are getting on to the real thing '—and in a sense they are right. But if they gladly allow themselves to become mere puppets in the hands of a dictator and enjoy it (as they well may), they forfeit a rewarding opportunity and experience. Of course, the teacher has often to ' play the children in ' to the business of production by example as well as by precept. But it is important that he should realise how little to do and when to stop and leave it mainly to the children.

There is also the danger of the teacher who does too little, who says, in effect, ' There's the play. Who'd like to play this or that part? Who'd like to be producer? All right, get on with it.' The teacher must always be ready to guide, and discussion will clearly be an important factor in working on a play text. Especially at first, children must be guided towards the truth of a play. Interpretations and certain production techniques, such as grouping and moves, have to be suggested. In fact, the teacher may have to do a certain amount of production himself at first, in order to set high standards.

Another danger of this transition period might be called ' the tyranny of the text '. Anything in print, even an advertisement, has a dangerous air of absolute truth about it for most children and many adults, and is liable to evoke an uncritical attitude. Teachers in particular need to beware of this. A false situation or a weak line in a text are still bad, even though they are in print, and, certainly in class-room work, the teacher should not hesitate to have them improved, if possible by the children. Again, stage directions may be a menace. In some editions of plays they will be the stage moves as used in a West End production. These are by no means sacrosanct, and what may be right for Shaftesbury Avenue is certainly not necessarily best for a class-room or school hall. Even the author's own directions may be unsuitable for class-room purposes. It is wiser to ignore all stage directions, except those referring to character. This is particularly necessary as a great majority of plays are written for a proscenium stage, and children have hitherto been playing in variations of ' the round ', with no thought of audience and ' fourth wall ' and may well continue to do so for a time.

Perhaps the greatest danger of all in this period is to think in terms of an audience too early. As soon as you think in terms of an audience all sorts of stage and acting technicalities must be considered, which should be left till later. Here again, the children may want to run before they can walk and be ambitious to get on to ' the real thing '. But the teacher would be wise to remember that if the children can wait until they are mature enough to learn these skills and then employ them as aids to expressing truth with sincerity and not as ends in themselves, then they will achieve far more far more quickly and far more effectively and significantly. In a way, work on a play in class-room conditions at this stage is similar to a school junior orchestra practising pieces of music, with no thought of future performance, but partly to learn something about orchestral playing, partly to improve their own skill, and mainly to enjoy the great satisfaction of playing together and playing a work of merit. The simile is not exact, obviously, for the class-room play demands a much greater degree of creative initiative by the actors and far less direction by the ' conductor ', but the objectives are alike. At this stage the text exists more as material for the children to use and enjoy in a purposeful and creative way than as a work of art to be treated with some reverence. Later, and particularly when they come to performance, communication of the truth of the text, important at this stage, will be the main consideration. But at the beginning of work on texts there should be little or no thought of performance.

What is the right age to begin work on texts? There is no right age; children should make this leap forward when they are ready; no earlier, no later. If they are reasonably intelligent and mature and if they have had plenty of experience of the kind suggested earlier, they may be ready for class-room work on texts at the top of the Junior School. The present writer would make only one exception to a general ban on Junior School performances of plays to an adult public—the Nativity play, for this is not so much a performance to an audience, as an act of worship in which everyone takes part. Some boys and girls may never be ready for texts. Some of the duller classes at the top of Secondary Modern Schools, for instance, may get more satisfaction from improvisation, movement, or dance-drama, in which they often excel. Sometimes these classes dislike the restrictions which a text may impose: they prefer to work out and act out their own adolescent ideas and emotions, and it will be more beneficial for them to do so. Further, their reading may not be fluent enough for them to read parts satisfactorily, nor their powers of memorizing adequate for learning lines.

What sort of plays should be used during the transition period and immediately after? It is probably best to begin with something that the children have written themselves, from their own improvisations, in which they will feel thoroughly at home. For there should be no sudden break in dramatic work; when children are ready they advance to the next stage which develops out of the previous one. However, there is another kind of home-made play which may have made its appearance earlier. Children often come up to the teacher and say, ' Please, may we do our play? ' On enquiry it proves that a small group, usually three or four, have devised and sometimes written, rehearsed and dressed their own play and wish to perform it to the class. It may be good or bad—these plays are often long and rambling; there is much talk, little action and frequent changes of scene—but the answer to the children's question must of course be ' yes '. No exception can be taken to an audience of the actors' contemporaries.

And after their own scripts? Here is the difficulty. There are hundreds of plays written for children and most of them ought to be burned. They are often trivial or futile, unexacting, undramatic, and abominably ' written down '. There are, thank goodness, some honourable exceptions, but not nearly enough. If only a few accredited playwrights would turn their hands to this work! However, some use may be made of these indifferent plays—they may serve as material for constructive remedial work. Under the guidance of the teacher the play may be altered for the better, and this process, though it will take time, may be a valuable exercise in critical thinking, play-construction and dialogue writing. And there need be little loss of time in starting to act the play. Passages can be tried out in action, discussed and altered, though later alterations will probably affect earlier scenes. This, however, can be turned to account, for it will help to impress the necessity for early ' planting ' of ideas which are to affect later action.

What are some of the characteristics of plays which are suitable for children at this stage of development? Obviously, they must be full of action, visible, externalized action, not internal tensions only, though they will be present inevitably; and no violence of an unpleasant kind—children are already over-exposed to violence by the so-called ' mass media '. The characters should not be subtle; black and white, rather than shades of grey; characters who are forthright, extrovert, who speak their minds, who take action and who are uninhibited, simple, but not childish. Probably most children at this stage of maturity will not want to play children, though this may not be so true of girls. Plots should be straightforward and full; the meagre and attenuated will bore. Speeches should be short, staging not too complicated, ' business ' straightforward. There should be a minimum of pure fantasy, a maximum of opportunity for bringing thought and imagination to bear on realistic or romantic-realistic situations. The writing should be vivid, strong and full of vitality and robust humour. Virtue should triumph.

What plays of this kind do we possess? Not many. Melodrama, certainly, though most nineteenth century melodrama will need drastic cutting of verbiage and occasional translation into more modern idiom. ' The Bells,' ' The Lyons Mail,' ' The Only Way,' 'A Tale of Two Cities,' ' The Prisoner of Zenda,' ' The Ticket-of-leave Man,' ' The Corsican Brothers,' ' Maria Martin ' and so on. These are honest-to-god, romantic stuff, and most of the children will still be at the romantic stage. Very different, but containing some of the characteristics suggested above, as well as peculiar qualities of their own, are the Miracle and Mystery Cycle plays. Noah's Flood, the Sacrifice of Isaac, much of the Shepherd's play (Towneley *Secunda Pastorum*), the Massacre of the Innocents are some of them. A selection suitable for schools has been published by Miss L. Feasey (' Old England at play '). ' Three Medieval Plays ' has been published by Mr. John Allen; There are also the various Mummer's plays (one is in Miss Feasey's collection). These last are perhaps the most likely link with the stage of improvisation. Children will play them ' dead straight ', without the painful attempts at burlesque to which adults are often tempted, and may achieve something of the sterling quality which these plays must have held for their original audiences. And members of the class who are not acting can enjoy some of the bucolic ' audience participation ' which must have characterised these performances. Some will consider one or two of the No plays to be suitable. ' Lady Precious Stream ' is a general favourite, but it will need judicious cutting: its imitations are generally rather feeble. 'The Bishop's Candlesticks' is an old chestnut, but will come fresh and movingly to children. A few other random suggestions are 'Tobias and the Angel', 'Jonah and the Whale,' 'The Pied Piper of Hamelin,' Clemence Dane's adaptation of 'Alice in Wonderland,' some Agatha Christie plays, Brian Way's adaptation of 'Pinocchio,' the adaptations of Dickens, 'The Speckled Band,' the adaptation of 'The Count of Monte Cristo,' 'National Velvet,' 'Treasure Island,' 'The Reluctant Dragon.' But plays suitable for children will be as much a matter of personal taste as any other choice in the world of the arts, and the only satisfactory way is for the teacher to browse through plays.

Here is one valid way of going to work on a play text (short or long) with a class. Tell the story of the plot to the class, with some hints as to character and climax. Discuss with them the main characteristics of the play. Either read the play to them, or make them read it to themselves. If the play is read to them, it should be an exciting and evocative reading, with very brief necessary explanations. Reading the play to them will probably be the quicker method and the more likely to make it live for them. After clearing an acting space, make groups improvise different scenes or sections of the play and have these improvisations acted consecutively. This will give further insight into the play, a foretaste of how the characters are to be acted and the situations handled. And the children will have begun action on it without too much delay. Next, take a section of the text, make the children read it to themselves, cast it, ask each member of this cast for observations on his character and the rest of the class for their comments on these observations. Now, have this section of the text improvised by the chosen cast. Then get decisions from the class as to the detailed setting of the scene on the acting space (probably chairs to mark entrances, chairs and tables to represent items of scenery, furniture, etc.), and appoint a stage-manager and assistant stage-manager to be responsible for the set and props. Tell each member of the class to start his own (simple) prompt copy in an exercise book and show them how to do it. You may want to do the same play with another class, so the actual texts (interleaved) should not be used. The whole class should enter each decision as to set, moves, pauses, etc., in his own prompt copy, with the necessary cues and page references. Now the teacher can go to work on the text, as if taking a rehearsal, but the sort of rehearsal which gives the maximum opportunity for the children to make decisions. At first the teacher should do a good deal of the producing himself to set high standards and given an example of the kind of job a good producer may be expected to do. After the children have rehearsed the first section of the play, the teacher should by question and answer obtain from the cast and from the rest of the class their comments on the production so far. ' Why do you think A says such-and-such at that particular point in the scene? ' ' What is B feeling towards C at this point? ' ' How do you know? ' ' What is X thinking here? ' ' How do you know? ' ' Would it be better if Y were close to X when he says such-and-such? ' . . . ' Why? ' At this early stage it is probably right for the teacher to insist on his point of view, in order to demonstrate sound ideas, and to keep this discussion short so that the children may continue with the acting. Then the children should rehearse the scene again to fix any alterations in mind and in the class's prompt copies. After this, a new cast should start improvising and rehearsing the next scene or section, followed by discussion and repetition, if necessary, of the scene, as before; and so on to the end of the play, changing the cast with each different scene or section. After going through the whole play once, further attention should be given to those scenes which have been least successful. Then a general discussion might be useful, followed, perhaps, by a second improvisation of scenes from the play done by different groups. Finally, a repetition of the whole play. If the play has caught the imagination of the class, the teacher may decide to work on it further and bring some scenes or the whole play to a state nearing performance, including the learning of parts; or he may choose to attack a new play, in the belief that the more good plays the children meet at this stage, the better.

This ' Rehearsal ' method of treating a play text is at least as old as Caldwell Cook at the Perse School. There are one or two further implications of this method to be discussed.

Acting with book in hand is always inhibiting. The only way partly to overcome this handicap is for the actors to become so absorbed in the play that the book becomes an aid rather than a hindrance. This is only possible when there has been thorough preparation, so that the players anticipate intellectually and emotionally the next speech, the next move, the next piece of action, the next situation, and perhaps invent their lines to some extent. This half-way stage between improvisation based on the text and reasonably accurate use of the text may help to preserve the original impetus and concentration; later, when, as the result of rehearsal, the words are coming more accurately, the children can have greater regard for the lines as written. But it is fatal to become ' book-bound '. So many people when reading a play keep their eyes glued on the text all the time and there is no inter-communication between the characters. It is difficult to avoid this when there is a succession of short speeches, but when speeches are longer it is easy to glance ahead for the next cue, put a thumb on it, raise the eyes and really take part in the scene. If really involved in the action and not too particular about the accuracy of the words, it is less difficult still.

Those not acting in a scene should regard themselves as co-producers. At convenient points the teacher should call a halt and invite comment; suggested alterations should be tried out then and there and discussed. Clearly, this all takes a good deal of time, and the teacher must be ready tactfully to end abortive argument and refuse trivial suggestions. The thing must continually progress. As the class become more experienced and more confident, suggestions are likely to become increasingly valid and discussion more protracted, and the teacher has continually to take the temperature of the class to ensure general interest.

If the class can prepare for a scene beforehand, much time may be saved. Some homework time should be available for drama. ' Next time we'll do scene 2. For homework, prepare this scene. Jones, you will play X, Smith, Y, Marilyn, Z, Sandra, W. Prepare the scene with the playing of your own characters in mind. Think out how you will say the lines; when and how you will move. All the others think of yourselves as producers—one of you will be called upon to produce—and prepare the scene accordingly. Plot out positions and moves on a piece of paper.' Soon the children will have the main responsibility for the production of their plays, and such homework will be increasingly necessary.

As with improvisations and acted stories, preparatory work in movement will be valuable, to get the mood of the play beforehand, or to enable a piece of action to run more smoothly, or to help someone to identify himself more fully with a character. Whenever movement is used the whole class should take part, if possible.

Unfortunately, ' doing a play ' in class often consists either of sitting at desks and reading parts, with questions and a running commentary from the teacher, or some children standing up, unprepared, with their books, in front of the class near the teacher's desk, in ' ever-coagulating groups ', reading the lines baldly, never moving, never raising their eyes from the text, occasionally being exhorted to ' put something into it '. (Put what into it?) This still passes for drama in many schools.

After this transition stage, the duration of which will be long or short according to the growing maturity and skill of the children, the development of the work will be characterised by the increasing difficulty and depth of the plays attempted, and by the increasing responsibility (under guidance) for the realisation in action of the texts by the children, and, perhaps, by the gradual introduction of the right kind of audiences.

There should be fairly rapid progress in the quality of the plays which the children work on. They should soon arrive at such plays as Tchekov's one-act ' The Proposal ', ' The Anniversary ' and ' The Wedding '; historical plays, such as Ronald Gow's ' Gallow's Glorious,' Drinkwater's 'Abraham Lincoln,' ' Oliver Cromwell,' ' Mary Stuart,' ' Robert E. Lee,' scenes and extracts from Hardy's ' The Dynasts ' (e.g. the Death of Nelson), ' Rose without a Thorn,' ' The Immortal Lady,' ' The Devil's Disciple,' ' The Lady with the Lamp,' ' Clive of India,' Barrie's ' The Boy David '; Lord Dunsany's ' The Night at an Inn,' ' Round the World in 80 Days,' further mystery cycle plays. And children can make their first contact with some of the great plays.

Extracts from Shakespeare, carefully cut, treated by the ' Rehearsal' method , should serve to whet the appetite for more. Simple scenes, the text of which is not too obscure and which make a unified whole, can be enjoyable and rewarding. The following re examples—the scenes from ' The Taming of the Shrew ' where

Petruchio has brought Katherine to his home (Act IV, Scene 1, beginning ' Petruchio: where be these knaves ' to ' exeunt Petruchio, Katherine, Curtis ') and Act IV, Scene 3 (to ' exit Tailor '); the murder of Banquo (' Macbeth ' Act III, Scene 3); the duel between Viola and Sir Andrew Aguecheek—the situation will need explanation—(' Twelfth Night,' Act III, Scene 4, from ' Sir Toby: Gentleman, God save thee ' to 'Antonio: I for him defy you! '); The Gadshill robbery (' Henry IV,' Part I, Act II, Scene 2); Hotspur's fight with the Prince of Wales (carefully cut) (' Henry IV,' Part I, Act V, Scene 4, from ' Enter Hotspur,' to end of scene); the Recruit scene from ' Henry IV,' Part II (Act IV, Scene 3, from ' Enter Falstaff ' to ' Falstaff: . . . by my troth, Master Shallow '; and from ' Reenter Falstaff and Justices ' to ' Falstaff: . . . lead the men away '); the death of Falstaff (' Henry V,' Act II, Scene 3 to ' cold as any stone '); for girls who learn French, the scene in ' Henry V ' where Katherine's maid teaches her English ('Henry V,' Act II, Scene 4); and our old friends the 'rude mechanicals ' from 'A Midsummer Night's Dream '. The teacher should explain the situations into which the scenes fit and briefly elucidate the text, where necessary, before beginning.

Methods at this stage will be similar to those of the transition period, except that the teacher will hand over more responsibility for interpretation and production to the children. The teacher will need to guide, by preliminary discussion and through preparatory work in movement, mime or improvisation; and if a producer or actor is wide of the mark, he must not hesitate to correct. It is as unwise to do too little, as it is to do too much.

It will have been appreciated that the kind of lessons just described might equally well be labelled ' dramatic literature ' as ' drama '. Certainly, the quality of the plays studied in this manner is and should be in no way inferior to the fiction or poetry which they meet in English lessons at this stage of their development.

But a play demands an audience. The children are probably ready now to play to an audience. (They may have asked for one several times). Why should not drama in the class-room have its audience, as well as drama on the school stage? The children are not mature or skilled enough yet for a fully adult audience, or a large one. Their first audiences should consist of their own contemporaries: one or two other classes and members of staff; a sympathetic audience, what might be called a ' domestic audience '. The play or scenes to be presented should fit into a lesson, and be performed in the place where they have been rehearsed. Simple costumes and ' props ' should have been improvised—they will make a great difference to the children—and should have been used in rehearsal for as long as possible. Parts should not be learned too early, not until the children are really under the skin of their characters, though they will have learned much of their parts already during rehearsal. There is no reason for the teacher to take on more of the production himself, or polish it up, just because the play is to be performed to an audience. The whole organisation of the performance should be left to the children.

As the children mature and their voices grow stronger they can play to larger audiences, but at no time should they have to strain their voices in order to throw them long distances. And not until towards the end of their school days should they play to mainly adult audiences of comparative strangers. First performances to other than a ' domestic ' audience could profitably be to a small audience in the hall, where they might act in the round on the floor with rostra and lighting, or in the ' three-quarter round ' against a background. Later still, they might use both stage and the floor of the hall, with the action flowing, if there are rostra or steps, from floor to stage and stage to floor. For boys and girls at school the last advance is on to the proscenium stage, and that only because they need all kinds of acting experience and because most school stages are uncompromisingly planted behind a proscenium arch; certainly not because there is any special virtue in the proscenium. Indeed, school-boys and girls are likely to communicate with greater sincerity and effect, if they are not unnecessarily remote from their audience.

The introduction of audiences of gradually increasing size and decreasing potential sympathy will necessitate serious attention to some simple stage and acting techniques. Some of these may have been considered before—for example, laughter, tears, stage falls and fights, the importance of varying heights. New techniques may be drawn from the children by the astute teacher who analyses current acting experience by means of leading questions. For example, it is obvious that the audience usually needs to see the actors' faces, particularly the faces of those who are speaking and those directly addressed; that when an actor is fidgetting about it is most distracting to the watchers; that when you are speaking to someone you usually look at them; that it will concentrate attention on the speaker if everyone else is looking at him (unless purposely otherwise). Children may not easily realise the boredom induced by monotony of speaking, and variation of pace may have to be explained and demonstrated. They may not understand that loudness does not necessarily indicate intensity of feeling, and that to feel the character's emotion within them is the surest way to express this intensity. (They are not professional actors who have experienced their character's emotions sometime ago at rehearsal and since then have been playing, admirably, no doubt, on technique). They may not yet know that movements and gestures to be convincing on the stage should usually be ' larger than life '. They certainly will not realise the importance of upstage and downstage positions. They will be ignorant of the significance of the proximity of characters to one another during different kinds of scene. Some of these technical matters may be grasped intuitively by children, others can wait till later; some may never be needed at all—the fewer, the better.

Unless they have already worked on verse speaking or choral speech, the introduction of an audience may be the first occasion on which conscious effort is made to rectify children's voices and speech—though they should certainly have had previous help. It will be a fitting time—the incentive to improve will be present— —and the aims will be that every word they speak shall be heard by their audience, that they can use their voices without strain, and that their speech may be vigorous, appropriate, incisive and pleasant. There will be no need for a great deal of technical training. But relaxation matters; movement should help here. Posture matters. Breathing matters. Flexibility of the jaws, the tongue and the lips matters. Clear vowels matter, and so do crisp consonants. Tone matters. These are all linked with each other; improvement in one should affect the others. But what matters most is confidence, ' meaning what you say,' or, in the case of playing a part, being

F

' inside ' that part—and plenty of practice. Variety and subtlety of inflexion, sensitive awareness of pitch should be the objectives, and these are often best achieved indirectly, so that the child concentrates on what he is saying, rather than how he says it. Children should aim at speaking low rather than high, at speaking comfortably and without strain or over-forcing, at speaking with pleasant tone, open jaw and, particularly, plenty of breath. A few minutes regular practice of, for example, combinations of consonants and vowels, of exercising jaws and tongue, of deep breathing, in fact of limbering up the vocal organs, as the body may be limbered up in movement exercises, before starting to work should gradually effect a very real improvement.

Some suggestions for plays (set down here in no special order) for children to work on as they mature are—' The Government Inspector,' ' The Boy with a Cart,' ' The Firstborn,' ' The Lady's not for Burning,' ' The Man born to be King,' ' Quality Street ' (girls), ' The Admirable Crichton ' (cut), ' The Rivals,' ' The Critic ' (Act II), ' The Importance of being Earnest,' ' The Birds,' ' The Queen and the Rebels,' ' The River Line,' ' Richard of Bordeaux,' 'Arms and the Man,' ' St. Joan,' ' Noah ' (Obey), ' The Lark,' some Quintero plays, ' Riders to the Sea,' ' The Knight of the Burning Pestle,' ' The Shoemaker's Holiday,' ' She stoops to Conquer,' ' The Barretts of Wimpole Street,' ' Dr. Faustus,' ' The Devil's Disciple,' 'Antigone,' 'Antigone ' by Anouilh,' 'Androcles and the Lion ' (but very sophisticated really), ' The Playboy of the Western World,' ' The Cradle Song ' (girls), ' Let my people go ' (Ian Hay), ' Cranford ' (girls), ' The Strong are Lonely,' some of Molière's plays in translation, Tchekov's one-act plays, ' The Italian Straw Hat,' ' Happy and Glorious,' ' Palace Plays,' ' The Monkey's Paw,' and the appropriate Shakespeare plays, especially the histories.

CHAPTER VIII

There are those for whom the reading of dramatic literature to themselves will be perfectly sufficient. Such is their imaginative insight, the subtlety of their ear, and their appreciation of language and character that they have little need to see a play performed or take part in it themselves. For most of us, however, the watching of or the acting in a play completes and fulfils our understanding of it; and particularly the acting in it. To have to speak the lines of a character in a play with truth, accuracy and rhythm demands a full knowledge, understanding and appreciation of the whole play. Further, our share in bringing a text to life helps us towards an insight into the mind of the author and the ideas which he wishes to convey which few can obtain by reading or watching alone. It gives us an extra dimension, so to speak.

The ' Rehearsal ' method suggested above, then, is for many, the most effective way of studying dramatic literature in the classroom; or, indeed, in the play-reading society. If the object of the latter is not mainly a social one, or a means of reading the maximum number of plays (which can be done in an armchair by oneself), but a real understanding and appreciation of a given play, then the preparation of a play as for performance will give the greater satisfaction. And the play rehearsed and read to an audience without costume or décor can amount to a near approximation to a full production for both actors and audience. The real meat of the play can be enjoyed. Most great plays were written to be acted and some for particular actors and particular theatres. Then let us act them, if we wish to relish and know and understand them fully; act them not necessarily for performance, but for our own enjoyment.

The present writer will not quickly forget a Fifth Form in a Girls' Grammar School at work on their G.C.E. play, ' Julius Caesar '. During the previous lesson they had reached the murder of Caesar and had read and discussed it with their teacher. In the next lesson two girls produced the others in this scene on the stage in the hall. From the very beginning the crowd brought the scene vividly to life, electrifying each other and the principals—too much so, in fact. The murder was effectively and neatly carried out, in spite of some awkward moves before and after; Brutus and Antony were clear and intelligent, but the crowd infused the whole scene with fire and authority—and confusion. Afterwards the producers gave their comments and instructions for the next run-through, and there were one or two spirited arguments with exuberant members of the crowd. At the end I asked producers which parts of the scene they were going to work on especially.

'Oh the crowd! They were hopeless! They distracted attention from the principals, and most of them hadn't a clue which side they were rooting for. After all, they are really the most important people in the scene, and they most know what they're supposed to be thinking. And that ghastly murder! Everyone falling over each other and none of the conspirators in the least bit mad against Caesar. . . .'

That was the way in which this School, which had a tradition of acted drama, prepared for their external examinations. And this was Caldwell Cook's method, though his boys dressed up in appropriate costume and had a special place for their dramatic literature, known as 'The Mummery'. They acted their Shakespeare, and by the time they had to face the examiners in the School Certificate (in those days) they had taken part in some 13 or 14 plays. In consequence, as two of his ex-pupils told the present writer, 'the School Certificate literature paper was a piece of cake'. It is good to know that Caldwell Cook's methods have been revived at the Perse. This method succeeds, because it demands the maximum of action, thought, imagination, responsibility and initiative from the pupils. They make the play 'their own'. They enjoy it. At the end they really know the play; it is a living part of them. This method is far more likely to give them a love for the great playwrights than the receiving of notes, the answering of questions, and the writing of essays. One trembles to think of the number of boys and girls in the past and to some extent, also, in the present who leave school with an abiding hatred of Shakespeare and all his works.

Except, perhaps, when preparing for examinations, it is not

necessary to cover every scene in, for example, Shakespeare. After explanation of their content some can be omitted altogether. It is sometimes helpful, especially with young boys and girls, to start with one of the main scenes and work outward, so to speak—for instance, the murder scene in 'Julius Caesar', the trial scene in ' The Merchant of Venice '. This arouses interest at the beginning. But this main scene should always be included in its proper place when the children go through the play as a whole. Some teachers will rehearse a cast in the selected scene and present it to the rest of the class before embarking on a play.

' How should I speak these lines? ' Or ' how should these lines be spoken? ' If the answering of these questions are continuously in the background of the minds of teacher and taught, then it follows that the full and complete truth of a play must emerge, as far as the boys and girls are capable of appreciating it—the structure and rhythm of the lines, their meaning, their relevation of character and of one character's effect on another, the relationship of the characters to the current situation and to the play as a whole, the gestures or movements that may accompany the lines, and the relationship of such movements and gestures to the stage picture as a whole. ' How should these lines be spoken? ' The answer is the ultimate criterion of the understanding of a text, as the ultimate criterion of the understanding of a poem is the way in which it may be spoken or read aloud. But with a play its realisation in action is essential to full appreciation and comprehension.

However, the truth of a play may be understood in different ways. One person will see a character or a situation in one light, another in a different light. What is to happen when the scene is acted? Is the producer or the teacher to impose his own ideas, or the lowest common multiple of everybody's ideas? If the play is for public performance, most producers will decide on a particular version of the truth and stick to it; in the class-room the teacher will be in a somewhat different position. He will be wise to allow the actors their own ideas of character, as far as possible, provided that these fit in with the agreed conception of the scene. If this cannot be done, then the teacher must be prepared to have the last word.

A variation in the class-room treatment of, for example, an

Elizabethan text is to work out how the play might have been acted on a contemporary stage, either with a model, or on the floor of the hall or some large space. Many children and many teachers are good craftsmen, and to make a scale model of the Globe, for instance, should not be insuperable and will be enjoyable. Small figures of the characters in the play, suitably painted or dressed, can be added.

To take one obvious example—' Richard II,' Act III, Scene 3, before Flint Castle, where the rebellious Bolingbroke enters ' with drums and colours . . . York, Northumberland, Attendants and forces.' The teacher might ask, ' Where do they enter from? Why? Where do the principals take up their positions? Why? What happens to the attendants and forces? '

Then, after some talk about the success of the rebellion, the text continues—' Enter Percy.

Bolingbroke: Welcome, Harry: what, will not this castle yield . . .? '

The teacher asks, ' Where does Percy enter from? Why? Where does Percy move, after entrance? Why? '

Percy discloses that King Richard is inside the castle, and Bolingbroke commands some lords to go into the castle and threaten the King with civil war.

' Go,' he says, ' signify as much, while here we march
upon the grassy carpet of this plain.'
' Where do the lords exit? Why? ' the teacher asks.

' March on,' Bolingbroke says later, ' and mark King Richard how he looks? (Parle without, and answer within. Then a flourish. Enter on the walls King Richard. . . .)'

' Who does the marching (if anyone)? Where do they march? Where does the King enter? Why? '

After some argument the King exits ' from above ' and two-and-a-half lines later reenters on the stage: it looks as though King Richard would have had to come down from the walls at speed.

This method does not entail merely the working out of a few

stage moves and positions, it means understanding the significance of the lines so that each character may be placed in such a position that the full import of his words may be communicated to the audience and to the other characters on the stage. And not a move on the stage should be made without close consideration of the motives which make the character move. Therefore, to work out the moves and positions of a play takes you deep into that play. This is particularly rewarding in a Shakespeare text with its paucity of stage directions, the historical interest and suitability for its purpose of the stage on which it was performed, and the profundity of the writing. Again, the boys and girls can ' be ' individual characters and can act as producer.

This plotting of the action of an Elizabethan or Jacobean play might also take place more realistically in the hall, the floor of which can be marked out to the exact size of, for example, the Globe platform. Chairs can be placed to mark the two entrance doors and the columns supporting ' the heavens '. The stage can be used (unsatisfactorily) for the lower gallery, but the ' inner room ' (if its existence has not been finally discredited) cannot be underneath the gallery. This will be a make-shift reproduction, but it allows the pupils to play on something of an approximation to an Elizabethan stage and to that extent to make the play more positively alive. They will certainly be enabled to appreciate the vast size of the Globe stage. Whether the pupils are working with a model or on an approximation to the Globe-style stage, one aspect of the drama of this epoch will become apparent, and that is the significance of the lack of pauses between one scene and another. King Richard goes off as Bolingbroke's prisoner at the end of one scene by one door, and straightaway Richard's Queen comes in on the opposite side of the stage to the poignant garden scene in which she learns that Richard has been deposed. After Antony has moved the citizens of Rome to take revenge on the murderers of Caesar and heard that Octavius, Caesar's heir, is in Rome, he exits: immediately, Cicero comes in to meet his undeserved death at the hands of the mob: directly they have surged out, the curtains of the ' inner room ' are drawn to show Antony, Octavius and Lepidus at a table. The first lines in this scene now take on added significance.

'Antony: These many, then, shall die; their names are pricked.

Oct: Your brother too must die: consent you, Lepidus?

Lep: I do consent—

Oct: Prick him down, Antony.

Lep: Upon condition Publius shall not live,
Who is your sister's son, Mark Antony.

Ant: He shall not live; look, with a spot I damn him . . .'

This piling of ruthless scene on implacable scene with hardly a moment's pause has to be seen to be appreciated.

There are two pieces of historical knowledge to which, one can be fairly certain, all children will be exposed at least once during their school careers—the three-field system and the Elizabethan stage. Both are interesting items of social history, both lend themselves to pictorial illustration; but why these in particular (plus a few others), and, especially, why only the Elizabethan stage? Much led up to Shakespeare; much has followed him.

Drama reflects the social, philosophical and perhaps political climate of the time. Playhouses reflect to a great extent the physical conditions demanded by the plays, as well as the architectural conditions of the time. Costume displays the peculiar forms of vanity current, and décor the prevailing theatrical ingenuity and artistic conceptions of the age. These can be fascinating by-ways for the historian and not without interest and value for the student of literature. The Greek theatre and the Medieval period are two obvious examples. Even a rather superficial consideration of Greek tragedy and comedy can provide some knowledge of Greek life, religion, superstition and philosophy. Greek theatres give evidence of local climate, building materials, architecture, sculpture. Both may involve some study of the festivals and the ways in which Greek drama developed. The growth of drama from the ' Quem Quaeritis ' to the Corpus Christi plays will introduce some of the fundamental concepts of medieval Europe, and the development of the playing space from church to pageant cart illustrates some of the social conditions of town life, as well as the increasing secularization of the drama.

Drama and its physical conditions provide a commentary on life as lived at certain times, at any rate, in the civilisation of the West, rather more fully, perhaps, than other forms of literature—for the novel is a comparatively recent growth, and Chaucers or Byrons are rare. Life, the whole of life, is as much the subject matter of the English teacher as of the teaching of history. For both, plays and the theatre, with their comment on contemporary life, can provide additional valuable material. The historian, especially, always hopes that his older boys and girls will find time to ' read round ' their subject: here is some relevant ' round-reading '. And some cooperation in respect of drama and theatre lower down in the school between English and history teachers may not be impossible.

CHAPTER IX

In one way the School Play is the culmination of a pupil's work in drama at school. In another way it is just a part of his educational progress which will continue throughout his life, and, in terms of drama, may lead him to a career in the theatre, to the enjoyment of an amateur dramatic society, or to intelligent and critical membership of audiences of the live theatre, cinema, radio and television.

The School Play is an important and unique school occasion. The School is on show. Local grandees, members of the Governing Body, friends of the School are among the mainly adult audiences. There is an air about the whole thing. It has to be as good as staff and boys or girls can make it, and sometimes it is very good indeed. Because the School is on show members of the staff usually take on the chief responsibilities—for choice of play, for production, costumes, décor, props, lighting. Pupils may help with sewing, painting, carpentry and the switch board; they may have some freedom in interpretation of parts and their suggestions concerning production may be adopted; they may undertake backstage and front-of-house responsibilities; but the main creative work is generally done by members of the staff. In a school where there has been a course of drama similar to that suggested in these pages, this is all to the good. It is beneficial for boys and girls to be well produced in a finely written play. It sets for them high standards of achievement in all the theatre arts; it shows them how the backstage mechanism of a production should be organised; it gives a considerable number of them a share in the responsibility for the success of the school's enterprise; it enables them to share in the cooperative creation of a work of art. And it may give to everyone connected with the school something to be proud of. In a school where there is little drama, association with the school play may be a very beneficial experience. The gradually increasing identification with an imaginary character in certain situations, the increasing sense of team spirit, of being part of something which is visibly growing around you, of being from time to time temporarily isolated in close partnership with others intent on the same objective; all these are valuable experiences, apart from other advantages mentioned earlier. But it is a pity that these experiences should be, so to speak, a head with little or no body to support and nourish it. A school play the actors in which (often an élite who ' act ') have had little or no previous progressive dramatic experience is rather like a sports day for which the athletes may have had only a few weeks' practice and training. It is liable not to be as interesting as the audience have the right to expect. Occasionally, indeed, it is an insult to them. And both athletes and actors may suffer from unnecessary strain, or an inflated opinion of themselves.

There should be little difference in principle between methods of going to work on the school play and on any other play acted at school in the class-room or elsewhere, except where the aim of setting an inspiring example of how to produce, how to design and how to organise necessarily throws greater onus on the teacher. But there should be all the preliminary work in discussion, in preparatory movement and improvisation; there should be experiment in production; and there should be a great deal of freedom of interpretation, subject to the producer's final decision. In short, the boys or girls should have the maximum opportunity for exerting a creative influence and for assuming responsibility, subject to the agreed conception of the ultimate truth of the play. Rehearsals should always be creative. The play should grow slowly at the hands of producer and cast; its truth should gradually emerge and be communicated through them.

A few miscellaneous suggestions, obvious to the experienced, follow for the benefit, perhaps, of the less experienced. The usual theatre procedures, for example, the annotated prompt copy, the stage-managerial responsibilities, the scenery and lighting plots, will make for efficiency and economy of time and effort. There are many books which give detailed advice on these and other facets of play production. The cast should rehearse with props and approximation to costumes (e.g. cloaks, long skirts, etc.) quite early in order to get used to them. As suggested before, there is an ideal moment for learning lines and for insisting that the cast should be word-perfect—and it is not too early and certainly not too late. It comes when the cast as a whole have mastered their moves, when they have some idea of the sequence of the dialogue and the structure of the scenes and have learnt some lines already through rehearsal, when they are beginning to show confidence in their parts, when their characters are beginning to take on real personality; when, in fact, their books are becoming an encumbrance. It is a difficult moment to decide and only the producer can make the decision. But once they start to learn, the sooner they cease to fumble for words the better, and the producer must be prepared to be rude to anyone who is not rapidly word perfect. And ' word-perfect ' means literally knowing the precise words which the author has written; he has chosen them with a purpose, ' near enough ' is not good enough. Ideally, rehearsals should be frequent, though this may be difficult to achieve at school. They should be frequent over a short space of time, so that the cast can be brought up to their best at the right moment. Timing of rehearsals and performances will, of course, vary from school to school. There will always come that ghastly stage when everything seems ' stale, flat and unprofitable ', and it is important to get through this stage in time for a ' second wind ' (mixing the metaphors) to take the cast with increasing power to the finishing tape. This is the moment when the producer probably has to be rude, exacting and stimulating. The cast feel and perhaps say, ' We are ready now'; the producer feels and may say, ' now we can really start to get somewhere. This is efficient, but dead. Now we can begin to breathe life into it.' There should be more than one dress rehearsal. The cast should rehearse with lighting and sound effects before the dress rehearsals. The official prompter should be present at all rehearsals, and mark all pauses in his copy. Soon after the beginning of rehearsals the cast should be instructed in the use of make-up, particularly for their own parts. They will enjoy this, and it is obviously better that they should make themselves up than depend on the staff. They can practise during the long periods of rehearsal when they are not on stage. Acting techniques should be kept to a necessary minimum—boys and girls do not need to ' play on technique ' for their three or four performances. The producer, of course, will not dictate: he will paint a word picture of the actor's character and the current situation and leave it to the actor. But to economise time he will dictate such essentials as major moves, entrances and exits during the earliest rehearsals. He will not attempt to make last minute alterations. He will be encouraging, serene, infinitely patient, and sometimes outrageously angry. His last words to his cast before performance will be something like, 'Attack it. Enjoy it.' And then he will go and sit in front and exercise patience, tolerance and humour.

One of the most successful school plays the present writer has ever seen was a performance of ' The Tempest ' by a Secondary Modern Girls' School. The Headmistress was keenly interested in drama and the speaking of verse and had built up an excellent tradition in the school. Work on the play happened twice a week after lessons and began nine months before performance. First, the girls read the play with the Head, who discussed and explained its contents very fully, and the circumstances in which it was first acted. After this, there was a good deal of discussion on how the scenes were to be acted, the different characters and how they were to be played. In rehearsal the Head almost always accepted the girls' interpretations of their characters and made but few suggestions as to production; she left most of this to the girls, even when she disagreed. The lighting, scenery and costumes were the responsibilities of the staff. The results in performance were extremely vital acting, clear and pleasant speaking, valid, but child-like versions of the characters—and insipid, sometimes vulgar costumes, lighting and scenery. There were two complete casts, each giving two performances. The play was brought vividly to life by these pleasant, but not very intelligent girls, under the wise and enthusiastic guidance of their Headmistress.

Audiences for the school play should be kept small and intimate, if possible—say 300–400. It is a considerable strain on boys and girls who are not used to it to have to project over the vast distances of some school halls, built to hold over 1,000 people. School actors should not have to raise their voices unduly, nor should their acting need to be larger than larger than life. They should be able to communicate easily to their audience and experience the delight of holding them. And the audience should be able to see and hear without difficulty.

A small theatre is the ideal, but so many school plays have to
take place in a huge hall, which the school authorities may wish to
fill for several performances in order to raise money. If the
primary object of the school play is the development of those
taking part, then size of audience or of box-office returns matters
little. It should be possible in a large hall to screen off the back of
the auditorium so that the actors do not have the depressing experience of playing to a half-empty house. Playing space and auditorium should be flexible so that any play may be performed on the
kind of stage most appropriate to it, and, if necessary, the action
can flow from stage to auditorium and back, or be played in ' the
round ' or ' near round '. The auditorium should be wider rather
than narrow, and the stage lower rather than higher, the seating
movable, the lighting apparatus flexible so that it may be able to
light adequately any portion of the theatre or hall, and there should
be generous off-stage and backstage space.   Flexibility and sim-
plicity should be the key notes of the design of stage and auditorium.   So many school stages are imitations of early West-End
stages, but without sufficient height over the stage, sufficient wing-
space, with radiators in the back-stage wall and with no room to
move ' behind ' from one side of the stage to the other. If architects
would take advice from members of staff, Drama Advisers and
others who know, much money and frustration would be saved.
Other things being equal, the last word on school accommodation
should be with those who have to use the place.

Parallel with the school play and, perhaps, even more valuable
from the point of view of pupils' development is the play produced
for an audience of contemporaries and friends by the older boys
and girls, in which all initiative and responsibility is theirs. Clearly,
these productions must be treated with great sympathy. Perhaps
the only place for guidance here is in the choice of play—in order
to save the pupils from themselves. Like some amateur companies,
they are liable to choose West-End successes, particularly farces or
subtle comedies, which are far beyond their powers. Otherwise
they should be left to make and profit by their mistakes, unless
they appeal for help.

CHAPTER X

' How do I start?'

The beginnings of dramatic work in school or elsewhere may present problems, except usually with young children, or older boys and girls or adults who purposefully seek instruction. For the former it is generally an extension of normal imaginative play; for the latter it is what they actively desire, but, even with them, there may be self-consciousness, inhibitions, or unconscious resistance to break down. For many children over the age of, say, 11 or 12, and adolescents and adults, even though they may be interested in and keen on the prospect of dramatic work, there are often these barriers of self-consciousness and inhibitions to overcome, particularly the fear of ' making a fool of myself in public ', of ' letting myself go ', with the consequent defence mechanisms of laughter and parody. Those whose task it has been to introduce adolescents and adults to any form of drama—movement, mime, improvisation, though less so with straightforward work on texts— have experienced moments of agony when chaos has seemed inevitable, or mocking indifference appears to be the sole reaction to one's increasingly desperate efforts. And it is hard at such times to remember that apparent lack of success may be due to a natural defence by the taught rather than to lack of skill on the part of the teacher.

The problem to be solved is simple to state, though not so easy to solve in practice. It is how to involve these boys or girls or adults mentally and imaginatively in this or that particular imaginary situation so that they may be concentrated upon their work and therefore tend to forget about themselves; and to do this frequently until it is natural to become absorbed in this new kind of work. The older the pupils, the longer the process will take, as a rule, particularly in the case of movement which so many Britishers initially fear.

Every teacher will solve this problem, as he should solve any teaching problem, in his own individual way to suit the needs of the particular group of children or adults in front of him. Once again, there are no correct solutions. There follow one or two suggestions for those who may require them—in addition to the ideas already put forward in the earlier section on work in Infant Schools.

In the Infant School, as stated above, drama is a form of play and play often takes a dramatic form. With older children in Infant Schools or younger children in Junior Schools a start might be made with a progressive sequence such as—stories and poems with ‘ refrains ’ in which the children join as the story is told or read to them (‘ I’ll huff and I’ll puff and I’ll blow your house down! ’); stories and poems with accompanying noises made by the children (‘ and the wind howled, and the rain spattered on the windows ’); stories and poems with noises, dialogue and actions, done by the children. Such use of stories and poems is common practice in Infant Schools, but some teachers do not realise that, amongst other achievements, they are, in fact, making a sound start on dramatic work. But so far all or most of the children have been sitting down during the telling of the story or speaking of the poem. Now comes the story or poem when all the children are, if practicable, moving about the room acting the story as it is told or read. For this purpose it may be necessary to divide the class into groups. (‘ The monks were all going about their daily work. Some were weeding the garden, some preparing vegetables for their meal, some cooking, some sweeping the corridors, some reading or writing or painting in their cells. But the Tumbler was standing on his head before the statue of the Blessed Virgin in the chapel’). As always, it will be advisable to do some preliminary practice of the actions required before the story begins. This last use of story or poem may be a fruitful beginning (at their own level) with pupils of any age, but the older the pupil, the more necessary is the preliminary practice.

The difficult stage with older adolescents and adults is to get them up on to their feet. They are less self-conscious when sitting (because not yet fully committed and physically and emotionally still close to each other, within the protective crowd, not yet individuals in isolation), and they will mime, or speak or sing in chorus quite happily, though defensive laughter and parody may occur. But sometime they have got to take the plunge and stand

and move in all their naked (so to speak) individuality in the bare and unsympathetic space around them. To make the plunge they have to become involved in an imaginative situation. Music, of course, is a great help at this crucial moment, so is strong rhythm, clapped or stamped by them, or beat out for them on a drum; both are aids to becoming relaxed and caught up in the imaginary situation of, for example, the story or poem being read or told. Some of Vachel Lindsay's poems with their marked rhythms and exciting content, for instance, can exert an almost hynpotic influence and have been found to be champion ' de-inhibiters '.

An effective start can also be made from movement or mime or certain acting techniques. It will often appeal to boys and girls of secondary school age to begin, for example, by learning stage falls. This piece of technique implies dramatic action of a sensational kind and carries with it a whiff of theatrical glamour (' like how they do it on the stage '). ' What could lead up to a stage fall? ' ' A faint, bad news, a fight, a shot.' ' What caused her to faint? ' ' Why were they fighting? ' ' Why did he shoot and kill? ' ' In pairs, work out a scene showing the faint, the fight, the shot, in each case bringing in a fall.' Here it is easy to go on to stage fights without weapons, showing how much more convincing is the kind of stage fight in which the fighters do not touch one another. Or the order of events might be stage falls, stage fights, scenes leading up to either the falls, or the fights and falls.

One or two examples of beginning from mime or movement. ' You are feeling your way down a long, dark passage. At the end of it you suddenly come upon . . .' (object purposely left to the imagination of the individual). 'At the end of this room is something you are uncertain of. Walk there cautiously, silently, and find out what it is. Then come back again, impressed with what you have seen, and begin to take some action about it. We should be able to tell from your action what you have seen.' Silence may be both dramatic in itself and a mighty aid to concentration. First lessons in drama are often most successful when quietness reigns, least successful when there is much noise (in real life fights are usually comparatively silent affairs). Then there are walking, running, starting, stopping exercises, which are normal, unembarrassing and quiet activities, and can lead to dramatic situations which may

G

be explored. ' Stand up. Walk slowly round the room. Faster. Faster. Slow. Slower. Slower. Stop slowly. Stand still. Still. Quiet. Close your eyes. Relax. Open your eyes. Start to walk as slowly as possible. Faster. Slower. Stop. There is someone following you. Look round slowly. He's there. Look back again. Walk quickly. Twist and turn. Try to throw him "off the scent". Slow down. Stop. Look slowly round. Is he still there? . . . In pairs, work out a scene about one person following another.' Or— first, indicate the 4 points of the compass, then . . . ' Stand up. Pace out 5 paces East; 10 paces North; 7 paces West. Take your spade. Dig. After digging for a while your spade strikes metal. You dig excitedly. Slowly you unearth a box. It is heavy. You lift it out with difficulty. You force open the lid with your spade. You find. . . . In pairs, work out a scene round this incident.' (All these instructions in a quiet voice).

There are many possible ideas of a similar kind. The pupils get up from their seats and are immediately involved in an ordinary activity leading to an imaginary situation which is potentially dramatic, or in an imaginary situation itself which demands normal activity but contains potential drama. They are all working simultaneously and to order and therefore have less opportunity for self-consciousness; and they are then asked to improvise on the basis of what they have already done. But it is important usually that the subsequent improvisations should be worked out and then acted simultaneously also.

If the pupils, of whatever age, are quickly caught up in an imaginary dramatic situation which demands quiet, concentrated action, the difficult beginning will have been effectively achieved. But it may be necessary for some time afterwards to do similar exercises, or (perhaps later) exercises in movement, to ensure concentration at the start of each lesson. Such exercises should be relevant to the ensuing work.

What can be done in a confined space, such as a small classroom containing rows of heavy, iron-clad desks?

Success in any dramatic work depends on the degree of absorption of the children and the extent to which they are quickened by the current imaginary situation: in short, on initial and continuous firing of the imagination. The present writer has seen teachers stimulate children to prodigies of inspired improvisation in rooms where the pupils had to move sideways down the aisles between desks. When the imagination is alight, space counts for less and less. It is possible to obtain a little more room for acting by using (where possible) the top of desks and the aisles between desks, but this is not really the solution. The solution is within; and, of course, in the material used. It is possible to mime at desks and to do a limited form of movement, provided there is real concentration on a well-chosen theme. Improvisations should be less difficult. There will be more need than ever for preliminary relaxation exercises and such preparatory movement exercises as are practicable, and preliminary discussion; for any activities which set mind and imagination working at full blast.

What subjects will be appropriate? Obviously, subjects which demand a confined space. A small class-room, for example; much drama could, and does take place within the four walls of a small class-room, but it should not bear too close a resemblance to normal life in the particular children's own school, otherwise it may be imitative and lack imaginative application. But there are class-rooms in other countries, class-rooms of fiction (at Dotheboys Hall, for instance), class-rooms of the past, class-rooms containing teacher and children very different from those found in the children's own school. Drama could, and does, happen in an aircraft—spies, smugglers could be identified and later arrested; revolutionaries or escaping prisoners hold up pilots and take over aeroplanes for their own purposes; there are crashes in desert or jungle, crash-landings on aerodromes, bomber crews in difficulties—the varied reactions of the different people involved and the drama (perhaps in the newspaper sense only) of the event and its consequences. Drama may occur, and does, in trains, underground trains, omnibuses, chars-à-banc, lifts, hospital wards. It happens in small, cramped rooms, where, for example, the prisoners of a dictator await trial or execution, or where escapers pause on their way to freedom or recapture, or victims of the dentist or doctor wait for their appointment. It was evident as the tricoteuses sat at the foot of the guillotine. Trials may be, and often are, highly dramatic. So are jury rooms. So are stormy meetings to discuss controversies. Some of these suggestions are sensational, but there is no need for the head-line subject. Where many people, or few, find themselves together for some time in a room, or any other space where movement is restricted, tension may be present or may be generated, and tension often means drama, and drama does not necessarily entail much physical action.

Unfortunately, there exists a tragically large number of children who are restricted in movement, temporarily or permanently. Some kind of dramatic work is possible and profitable for many of them. Schools for the physically handicapped perform plays, sometimes of a quality which makes their audience forget their handicap. The deaf derive enjoyment and benefit from mime and movement, act plays and do speech work in dialogue. The blind play games and do gymnastics; almost the whole range of dramatic enterprise would seem to be open to them. Many children in bed in hospital may be perfectly capable of certain kinds of mime and movement, improvisation and work on texts. With fire in the belly children can do much, provided that their circumstances are not completely inhibiting.

Many schools hold House or Form play competitions and festivals, in which, again, the boys and girls have full responsibility. Sometimes, when there is a tradition of drama in the school, the results are good: where there is no such tradition they may be deplorable—and it cannot help anybody to be content with the second-rate. If education aims at anything, it aims at the achievement of the excellent. Sometimes, too, the whole enterprise is bedevilled by the award of a cup, or similar prize, and a public assessment by an exernal adjudicator. As soon as the spirit of competition enters into a festival of the arts for young people it is likely to be tarnished. The judgment of the adjudicator—however skilled—is bound to be subjective. If an ' outsider ', he cannot know the native calibre of the different teams and which really deserves credit for surpassing normal achievement. The motives of those concerned with the productions may be contaminated by the desire to win the prize, and standards may suffer from unnecessary tensions. The critical judgment of the audience of boys and girls may be prejudiced; and the more patriotic, the more prejudiced. This audience may be over-influenced by the comments of the adjudicator, and, however true they may be, his hearers may adopt his views uncritically.

The arts should need no artificial boost. They can be enjoyed for their own sake. A festival by its very name implies something to be enjoyed. Let the Houses or Forms or groups of boys and girls combine to provide a couple of hours' entertainment, at best something notable and memorable, for the sheer happiness of doing it or watching it.

CHAPTER XI

No one who reads this book is likely to quarrel with the idea that it is important for several obvious reasons to bring children, younger and older, into contact with the ' live ' theatre, both for their own sakes and for that of the theatre of the future. The more intelligently critical of the theatre the children can become, the better for everyone.

There are a number of companies, or other institutions, here and abroad, which give regular performances to children, and others which do so spasmodically. Some companies have been doing this for many years. There has always been controversy whether to bring the children to a theatre, or bring theatre to children. There is much to be said on both sides. The present writer inclines to the belief that for Primary School children theatre should be brought in to the school, and that Secondary boys and girls should go or be taken to the theatre, where and when this is practicable.

Young children are apt to be a particular kind of nuisance in a theatre (so may Secondary School boys and girls in a different way) and a considerable responsibility for those who conduct them. It is arguable that for some young children the theatre and its magic is apt to be overwhelming and to make too formidable an impact on the sensitive and highly imaginative. There may be too much, even for the present sometimes over-sophisticated and over-indulged Primary School child, to be assimilated at once—the glamour of the theatre itself, the demands of the performance, as well as the unfamiliarity of the whole experience. Emotional indigestion may well be the consequence. These children need the simple, and they need it in the security of their own familiar surroundings. They already have an over-rich diet of entertainment —television, radio, cinema—but the live theatre can be even more stimulating and exacting than these. This is not a matter of underestimating their capacity or their capability; it is a matter of over-feeding. Besides, a valuable element in theatre for young children is ' audience participation ', and, except, to some degree in pantomime, this is frowned upon in most theatres, even at special performances for children. Further, the sort of plays appropriate for children of this age should not require the elaborate equipment of a theatre. The closer the actors are to an audience of young children, the better. Proscenium stages merely separate, and direct personal communication suffers. Most young childern will not think of the actors entirely as actors playing parts, but, to some extent also, as real people. They can have their magic and the reality simultaneously, equally convinced by both. Theatrically, they have their cake and eat it: they have little disbelief to suspend. For the full effect of this the actors need to be close and on the same physical level.

But older boys and girls are ready to assimilate everything the theatre, with its pomp and circumstance, has to give. They can bring some critical sense to bear. They will not be as whole-heartedly committed as the younger ones. They have grown out of ' audience participation ', and their form of ' participation ', if any, is apt to take a different and unpleasant form. They want to be treated as adults, to undergo adult experiences, of which theatre-going is one. But they are ready to be caught up and exploited by the magic of the theatre and at the same time eager to see ' how it works '. Some companies playing to children will conduct parties of them backstage after the performance and explain to them how everything is done. So these children too can have it both ways. But the magic of the drama remains for its short hour, and it can probably exist more potently in the theatre than elsewhere for older boys and girls, as for their elders. If possible, no one should be denied this unique form of happiness, and for many children the opportunities provided by their school for going to the theatre are the only opportunities they will ever have.

The problem of what kind of plays children of different ages should see is as difficult as that of the plays they should act. In general, it is perhaps true that the same sort of play which is suitable for them to study and act in the class-room or in perform-ance, or the plot of which is appropriate for improvisation, is also suitable for them to see and enjoy. But many children can appre-ciate plays which they could not act satisfactorily. This does not mean, cf course, over-sophisticated or too subtle plays, nor plays in which the main ideas are utterly beyond them, though these qualifications may be modified if there is plenty of action. Many of the speeches in 'Macbeth' may be unintelligible to children, but they may be thrilled by the play. It is like their reading; if the thought is reasonably clear and there is plenty of action—not necessarily violent action—they will enjoy books which we may think far too adult. There are various levels at which play or book can be appreciated, and children may enjoy at their own level works which adults enjoy at a deeper level. A good story, plenty of tension and action, and rich rounded characters seems to be the recipe again. Some children's companies wisely have their plays specially written for them. Some companies make a point of putting on the G.C.E. plays, whether from kindness of heart or box office motives, and many boys and girls see these. It must obviously bring the play to life for them. Some schools make a point of sending parties to the theare at least once a term, a most praiseworthy practice, and a number of Local Education Authorities organize performances for school children.

Visits to a theatre of large crowds of Secondary boys and girls for special performances are sometimes a great mistake. Bus loads arrive in a state of some excitement (it is a change and a couple of hours ' off '), their excitement increases when they are inside the theatre, they shout and rag about, during the play they laugh or snigger at the wrong moments, and any mention of ' love ' is greeted with wolf-whistles and guffaws. Of course it is not always like this, but sometimes the behaviour is acutely embarrassing and most unfair on the actors. If school parties make up a section of a normal audience, their behaviour is usually good. Local Authorities would spend their money more wisely if they booked batches of seats for normal performances, whenever there is a suitable play. Ideally, the best way is for adults to take children to the theatre *en famille*.

Good plays for Primary School children to see are even more difficult to find than those for Secondary Schools. It seems far better that the company should write or improvise its own play, or have a play specially written. There is much to be said for a kind of Commedia dell 'Arte play, especially as the participation of the audience may demand a flexible script. A company which played much in West Country schools would base its play on a first-rate story for children, and at intervals would ask the children for a solution to some problem in the course of the play. ' What shall I do now? ' the character would ask, and would hold discussion with members of the audience. Sometimes the actor would talk the children round to a solution which fitted in with the script. Sometimes he would adapt script to suggestion. This small company took the minimum of props and costumes into the schools. They used what they found in the school, and a top hat or a head-dress was sufficient to signify a character. The rest was left, very rightly, to the children's imagination. In plays for Primary School children fantasy should be of a realistic kind. Devoid of humour and day-to-day matter-of-factness, fantasy tends to cloy; but the ' off-realistic ' may be entrancing. Simple characters with great definition and one or two outstanding personal traits seem to satisfy most. Plots can ramble, provided there is plenty of straightforward action.

Audience participation is sometimes dragged artificially into plays for Primary Schools. This would seem to be a mistake, for many proper occasions will arise naturally. Sometimes, too, companies may succumb to the temptation to have the whole audience screeching at them, pantomime-wise. ' Look out! 'E's be'ind yer! ' The audience should participate with complete sincerity and some subtlety. The author remembers vividly how some Junior School children were induced to mime by one actor.

' Take these boxes, will you? ' Imaginary boxes were handed out, taken and held. ' I think one of them contains the treasure ! Now, will you open your box carefully.' Imaginary boxes were gently opened. ' Now, look inside. Has your box got the treasure inside? ' ' No.' ' Yours? ' ' No.' And so on. None of them contained the treasure. ' Where can the box with the treasure be? ' ' It might be in that box over there on the rock.' The actor crosses, picks up an imaginary box, opens it. A grin of delight. ' Yes! Here it is. See.' And he holds out the imaginary box. ' What can you see in it? ' ' Gowld.' ' Silver.' ' Rubays.' ' Emeralds.' ' Diminks.' ' Take them out and show them to others, and then put them back, please.' The imaginary jewels were passed round, admired and put back. Such is the power of imaginative absorp-

tion. There was the usual chase through the audience. ' Hold them
up with your guns when they come round that way!' Children
brandished imaginary revolvers or sub-machine-guns and the
bandits were captured. When it was time for the interval and the
children were to go out into the playground for ten minutes, the
two characters on stage went to sleep, the producer came in and
whispered loudly, ' Tip-toe out, will you, so as not to wake them
up.' When it was time to restart, the two actors took up their
positions again and went to sleep, the children tiptoed in and settled
down in silence. Then the actors woke up and the play continued.
It was a brilliant device for getting the children in and out in
quiet order and for re-imposing concentration for the second half
of the play—and real audience participation.

Effective audience participation of this kind depends mainly
on the degree of concentration of the actors. If they are completely involved in the play, the children are likely to be also, and
so when the children are asked to take part they will do so with
absorption. There will be no showing off, no pushing others out of
the way. Such participation will add to the play for actors,
participators and the rest of the audience. After it is over the
participators may hardly be conscious that they have taken part.
Plays for Primary Schools to see should be similar to the acted
stories which the children will work on themselves, and one
criterion of success may be that they will act the whole play again
for themselves in their leisure time. However, too much audience
participation can be a mistake. The children are there to see a
play, not to help to make one. They should be enjoying plenty of
opportunity for the latter; now they are having a different experience—and in its own way an exacting one. After the play there
should be no ' follow-up ', except in casual conversation with the
children. Let them enjoy the performance and leave it at that. It
will have been a deep and memorable experience for some of them;
to write or talk unnecessarily about it may be spoil it for them.
Let it sink into them: if they want to, they will use it again in some
form or other. A composition about the performance will probably
bring forth nothing of merit. ' I liked it best when . . .'

Who is to play to children—professionals or amateurs? Clearly
whoever acts for children must be highly skilled in his art, and

sufficiently sympathetic and humble to immerse himself in a part and in a play which does not make great demands on his intelligence or his emotions. He must be able instantly to enter into communication with and forge bonds with children, without ' playing down '. He must have great energy, vitality and clarity. And it goes without saying that he should be fond of children. This seems to add up to the young professional or the teacher who is a very skilled amateur actor. Some students and ex-students of drama schools, who are training or have trained as teachers, do it very well. But probably, like teaching, it should, ideally, be a vocation.

CHAPTER XII

The fundamental problem is who are going to train the teachers? Potential teachers of drama in schools receive appropriate but insufficient instruction in some training colleges, and training in speech is too often perfunctory. To teach these future teachers properly the colleges need experts on their staff. Such experts should know a great deal about all the arts of the theatre, about the voice and speech and the underlying anatomy and physiology, about poetry, about the speaking of poetry, about dramatic literature, the history of drama and theatre, the history of costume, furniture, architecture, about social history in its many aspects, about movement and mime—apart from knowledge of children and how they learn, and knowledge of how to teach their own subjects. All this presupposes able tuition and much time. Acting alone, genuine achievement in which can come only through hours and hours of practice and experience, needs a vast amount of time, for the personality has to develop, and maturity comes slowly. An actor grows, and all growth is slow. Technique may be learnt swiftly, but acting is far more than technique. Production cannot be learnt; it depends partly on imaginative *flair*, partly upon experience—and experience consumes time. Again, a voice cannot be properly trained under three years' hard work. The teaching of any subject can only be learnt after much experience, and any deep knowledge of children must be the fruit of years of contact with them. Training the trainers of the teachers demands a great deal of time.

Unfortunately, the Schools and Colleges of speech and drama, which train the teachers from whom training colleges will draw their experts, are far too few in number. The annual output amounts to less than 100 teachers each year. Before they can enter training colleges they must have some years of teaching experience. There is considerable wastage after training. In addition to these, a small number of ex-training college students do a year's course in speech and drama which is valuable for their work in schools, but insufficient by itself really to qualify them for the position of expert. Then there are the external diplomas in speech and drama awarded by some colleges of drama, which, again, do not by themselves really qualify the holder to train teachers. Finally, there are the gifted ' amateurs ' employed by a few colleges who may or may not excel in training voices, actors, producers, and teachers of drama in schools. At most the total annual output of these potential trainers of teachers does not amount to 200, which is hardly sufficient to give the thousands of students now in training the necessary time to improve their voices alone.

The future is bedevilled by the fact that there is a very influential school of thought which believes sincerely, though ignorantly, that for teachers of spoken English (or speech and drama) a two years' course at a specialist college plus a year's course in teaching will be sufficient. Such courses would be sufficient for teaching spoken English in a school, as would a two-year course at a training college plus a year's course at a specialist college. But this is clearly quite inadequate as a basis for training teachers, for which a specialised background knowledge is essential.

The teacher's voice is of the utmost importance. It is his chief weapon. Loud or harsh or flat monotonous voices, day in, day out, can be fatal to fruitful communication between teacher and taught. It requires regular and continuous work under an expert to improve the voice. Further, the great majority whose voice and speech are normal may need the knowledge and practice which will enable them to project their voices, to set an example of good speech, to speak always with clarity and pleasant tone, to talk frequently and continuously over the weeks without undue strain—and to notice the children whose voices or speech need special attention. Almost all training colleges are conscious of the importance of the voices and speech of future teachers, but few of them can afford the time necessary to effect real improvement in this vital matter—there is so much else to be done—and by no means all of them can afford one specialist in spoken English in their staffing ratio, far less the two or three who may be necessary if all students are to receive adequate attention and help. There is some hope to be gained, however, from those Institutes of Education which demand a ' pass ' in speech from their students, as well as from the Examining

Bodies which set a test in oral English in G.C.E. And of course there are a number of colleges where work in spoken English is of high quality—but not nearly enough.

The training in speech and drama at training colleges should be mainly indirect—through the doing, as in schools. Apart from individual remedial work, the voice and speech of the students will be improved mainly by the speaking of verse, by acting parts, by making speeches, by telling stories to children, and so on, and by the techniques incidentally useful for these purposes. Some knowledge of acting, production, design and making of costumes, props, scenery, of lighting, of stage-management, of make-up will come through work on plays, often for performance. Experience in mime, movement, improvisation, acting and production will bring knowledge of these aspects of drama, and at the same time will give suggestions for work in schools. Knowledge of drama and the theatre and their history and development, of costume, décor and their development will probably come through directed personal reading. In addition, there will be some general guidance as to the development of dramatic work of all kinds in schools, its relationship to the subject of English, and its value for children as an art-form. The work in drama in training colleges will have two coordinated aims—the personal development of the student through the practice of this art, and the development of children through the practice of this art, and the methods by which this may be achieved. There will be similar personal and professional aims for work on voice and speech.

There can be no doubt that training in the arts, including that of drama in all its aspects, tends to produce students who are unusually lively personalities, alert, observant, full of ideas and self-confidence, sensitive and full of vitality, many of them just the sort of people to stimulate and inspire children. Of course, they are likely to be that sort of person to start with, or they would not specialize in the arts. But it is noticeable that even short exposure to the arts, including that of drama, tends to have a relaxing, loosening-up effect on quite ' ordinary ' adults, who sometimes become de-inhibited at an alarming rate.

In many training colleges all students receive suggestions as to how to organize and conduct drama in schools, but, apart from those taking a main or subsidiary course in drama, there is often little practical work. Skill in an art or in the teaching of an art can be learnt only through the practice of the art or the practice of teaching it. You cannot effectively teach mime or improvisation, for example, unless you have experienced the doing of them. You may not be very good yourself, but that need not make you a poor teacher. You must, however, be something of an enthusiast. There are a number of enthusiastic, but indifferent cricketers who are first-class coaches. In some colleges the dual conception of drama—as an art-form and as an integral part of the subject of English—is not realized. Members of the speech and drama staff are, in fact, members of the English staff, and both staffs should cooperate fully—and sometimes do, with admirable effect. Nevertheless, it is gratifying to remember the great strides forward made by the training colleges in the whole world of spoken English. And the solution is—as always—to get the right people on the staff and give them sufficient time. The ideal is the English graduate who has done a fullish course of speech and drama, or the fully trained ex-student of a School or College of speech and drama who is very widely read and an experienced teacher of all branches of English. These are rare birds.